Tom Montgomery Fate

D0109968

CABIN FEVER

A Suburban Father's
Search for the Wild

Beacon Press ?& *Boston*

Beacon Press
25 Beacon Street
Boston, Massachusetts 02108-2892
www.beacon.org

Beacon Press books
are published under the auspices of
the Unitarian Universalist Association of Congregations.

15 14   8 7 6 5 4 3 2

Text design by Jody Hanson at Wilsted & Taylor Publishing Services

Library of Congress Cataloging-in-Publication Data
Montgomery-Fate, Tom
Cabin fever : a suburban father's search for the wild / Tom Montgomery Fate.
p. cm.
ISBN 978-0-8070-0098-4 (paperback)
1. Sustainable living—United States. 2. Alternative lifestyles—United States.
3. Self-reliant living—United States. 4. Green movement—United States.
5. Environmentalism—United States. 6. Conservation of natural resources—
United States. I. Title.
GF78.M66 2011
333.72—dc22   2010049876

"Where Does the Temple Begin, Where Does It End?"
reprinted from *Why I Wake Early,* by Mary Oliver. © 2004 by Mary Oliver.
Reprinted by permission of Beacon Press, Boston.

For my parents,
Russell and Delores Fate

The question is not what you look at, but what you see.

HENRY DAVID THOREAU, *Journal*[1]

Contents

Author's Note

As Henry David Thoreau so beautifully demonstrates, a nature memoir is a work of art more than science, as much a spiritual endeavor as an intellectual one. And this influenced how *Walden* was written, and how it is "true." Though it is structured as if it took place in one year, Thoreau lived at the pond for two (1845–1847). And some events and key ideas in *Walden* stem from the seven years after Thoreau left the pond, as he continued working on the manuscript and preparing it for later publication (in 1854). In short, *Walden* condenses about eight years of Thoreau's life into the literary frame of a single year.

Likewise, the events in this book took place not in one year, but during the four years I spent working on it. One of those years I had a sabbatical, during which I roughed out about half the text. In spite of this method, I've tried to make the book as accurate as possible by keeping the events "in season," as they occurred, and by relying heavily on my journal for details. But even so, remembering events and people remains a subjective and interpretive process. Memory requires the imagination, and it can engage both the intellect and the emotions. The relationship between "facts" and "truths" is rarely as clear as we want to believe. In order to "protect the innocent," I have also changed some names here. But not my family's, of course, to whom I remain indebted for allowing me to write so openly about their lives.

Deliberate Life
A Search for Balance

As travelers go round the world and report natural objects
and phenomena, so faithfully let another stay at home and
report the phenomena of his own life. . . .

HENRY DAVID THOREAU, *Journal*[1]

One sunny afternoon a few years ago, I drove to southwest Michigan to build a cabin in the woods. It was spring break, and I had just reread *Walden,* Henry David Thoreau's nineteenth-century account of his life in the woods at Walden Pond. The famous hermit-philosopher had again inspired me, but it was different from the first time I had read it: I was not an idealistic nineteen-year-old college freshman, but a harried and married forty-six-year-old father of three in suburban Chicago. Different things mattered. The book called me with more urgency—from my distracted middle-class, middle-aged life into the wild solitude it conjured.

That same morning, before leaving, I discussed the weekend with my wife, Carol, packed food and clothes, and then went to the garage to look for tools. When I pushed the remote and the garage door hummed open, I abruptly recognized my life: a wild tangle of bicycles and strollers and grilling utensils and patio furniture and wet cardboard boxes full of moldy books and kids' clothes. Amid the clutter, I found an old spade, two sawhorses, a metal tool box, and a post-hole digger, all of which I tossed into the back of our minivan. On the two-hour drive to Michigan that day, I recited Thoreau's mantra—"Simplify, simplify"—as a kind of prayer, thinking it might offer me some guidance. But it never really did.

We finished the cabin in two years—or at least stopped working on it then. Cobbled together with the help of family and friends, and with more patience than expertise, we built it on a fifty-acre plot of woods and meadow we own and share with six other families, friends from our old church. They bought the land cheap thirty years ago—a farm abandoned after a fire. It has since been slowly restored: the stone farmhouse rebuilt, thousands of pines and oaks planted, a large garden dug. And we maintain a network of walking trails that wind throughout the property.

Were he alive today, Thoreau might have little interest in our experiment in Michigan. But he might be a bit curious. He did, after all, anticipate those readers who would naively aspire to his ideals. In the first chapter of *Walden,* he addresses the relevance of his stint in the woods for the interested novice: "I would not have anyone adopt my mode of living . . . but I would have each one be very careful to find out and pursue *his own* way."[2]

Even when no one would buy his books, and long before there were Thoreau wannabes, he advised readers to listen for their own drummer, and find their own way through the forest. *Walden's* continued appeal is partly due to a romantic longing to get back to nature. And while Thoreau himself is also deeply romanticized, his commitment to the environment, his material self-sufficiency, and his less-is-more economics could not be more relevant. Such ideas resonate in a high-tech, high-speed culture, which excels at making waste and war. We have bifocal contacts and laser eye surgery but still struggle to see in the way Thoreau imagined—to find the essential balance of the I and the eye, of self and world. This is why, despite the vast distances of time and culture, I can't help but read Thoreau's artful interrogation of his life at Walden Pond as both a critique of my own and as an invitation to a new kind of vision, to the joy of enough in a culture of more, to a *deliberate* life.

That's what I'm seeking here: a more deliberate life. But *deliberate* doesn't just mean "intentional" or "careful"; it means "balanced." The word is tied to *libra*—the two-pan scale of justice, which is for weighing and balancing things—ideas, fears, love. Or maybe garlic: I saw such a scale once at a market in a tiny French village. The farmer put a hundred-gram weight in one silver pan and a handful of garlic in the other. The standard, or known weight, was balanced against the unknown. In this case the garlic was too heavy, so the pans didn't level. But the vendor gave it to me anyway, balancing the scale with his generosity. Deliberation is a creative act, an art.

My seven-year-old son, Bennett, sometimes tries to balance himself on the creaky iron fulcrum of a wooden teeter-totter at the playground. He jumps up on the heavy plank and puts one foot on each side of the center. Then he shifts his weight, pushing one end of the plank down, causing the other end to rise. He tries to stay balanced and level but can't for more than a few seconds. One side always starts to teeter up or totter down. He doesn't stay centered, but neither does he ever fall off. This struggle for balance, the rising and falling between earth and sky, gives him great joy. And he gives that joy to me, if I'm paying attention.

To put it plainly, a deliberate life is a search for balance—in mind and body and spirit—amid our daily lives. And though some might like to do that searching all alone in the woods, few can. Other "natural" commitments conflict: children, a partner, a job or two. Most readers who admire Thoreau's ideas don't have the freedom or desire to live a solitary life in the woods. Still, what many of us *do* want, and what this book is about, is finding a deeper connection to Nature in our ordinary lives—by seeking relationship and refuge *wherever* we find ourselves—whether it be on a walk through a forest preserve, on a family camping trip, or catching grasshoppers in the backyard.

"I have traveled a great deal in Concord," Thoreau famously wrote. For him, travel writing *was* nature writing, and it was local.

His search for the Wild was on home ground: an outward physical journey and an inward spiritual journey conducted not in pristine isolation, but on the humble Concord woodlot available to him.[3]

This point is vital for those who seek a more deliberate life today. Because since Thoreau's invention of the nature memoir 150 years ago, much of the natural environment itself has been destroyed. So the task is no longer to discover and record the rare, but to recover and nurture the ravaged—to try to restore some balance where we live. This is particularly true here, amid the Midwest's decimated woodlands and farms and its sprawling suburbs, where developers and nature often collide.

Every day I see these collisions—the imbalance—between humanity and the other animals that live here. Herons nest on our E. coli–choked river. Coyotes hunt on the runways of O'Hare International Airport while roaring jets land. A Canada goose gets trapped in the entryway of my office building. Rabbits nest in wood chips beneath a metal slide on a suburban playground. A wild cougar is gunned down in an alley by a Chicago policeman. Who belongs where? Who will take care of whom on this shrinking planet? How will we find the balance we seek?

These questions point to the structure of this book, and to my simple premise that we always live in between—forever teetering on the rusted fulcrum of our wondrous but uncertain lives. Each chapter attempts to deliberate two ends of some scale of human experience: instinct and reason, nature and technology, love and sex, childhood and parenthood, nature and religion, art and activism, and others.

I offer not answers, but stories, which are meant to point readers back to their own, and to one of Thoreau's central tenets: learning to see the beauty and relatedness of the *wild without*, in the woods, is not separate from learning to see the beauty and relatedness of the *wild within* ourselves, and in our partners and children. Because although we humans are often estranged from nature by our intellect and appetites, we all still belong to it—in brain and breath, in birth and death—no matter where or what or who we call home.

Home. That's where I'm headed. This is an invitation to the way-finding. These words are tracks through a sun-dazzled meadow and a long winter night full of coughing children. They follow ants and cicadas and coyotes and the sudden twists and turns of love and marriage. They disappear for a while in a swamp but re-appear along the bank of a small, polluted river. Sometimes they may grow faint or double back. So if you lose them in a thicket of buckthorn, or if they end at the water's edge, just look for them somewhere on the other side. Or perhaps find another trail you hadn't noticed before. Or do what Thoreau did: walk straight into the thorny bramble and make your own.

SPRING

If a man does not keep pace with his companions,
perhaps it is because he hears a different drummer.
Let him step to the music which he hears,
however measured or far away.
It is not important that he should mature
as soon as an apple-tree or an oak.
Shall he turn his spring into summer?

HENRY DAVID THOREAU, *Walden*[1]

Chapter 1

Picking Blackberries
Nature and Technology

Time is but the stream I go a-fishing in. I drink at it; but while
I drink I see the sandy bottom and detect how shallow it is.
Its thin current slides away, but eternity remains. I would drink
deeper; fish in the sky, whose bottom is pebbly with stars.

HENRY DAVID THOREAU, *Walden*[1]

After a storm passes over the woods, I open the cabin windows. Rain drips from a roof corner onto a fist-sized piece of granite. Over decades, the drip can wear a hole through the rock. I have seen such holes beneath a roof on a cobblestone street in London, and beneath a waterfall in the White Mountains. But though even solid rock yields to the water's ticking patience, to the timeless rhythm of nature, people don't. We don't live by the drip-tick of water on stone, or the cycle of sun and moon. Our species has almost triumphed over these primitive gauges of time. Time is less a stream we go a-fishing in, a mystery to which we belong, than a commodity that belongs to us.

Last week I stumbled on a display of pricey cast-iron sundials in a garden store. But the fifty-pound, prerusted yard ornaments no longer mark time; they cast shadows few know how to read. Now, when men lose their hair, or their erections, they take drugs to bring them back. Pregnant women, evading the clock of their own bodies, can schedule their births for a convenient day—to fit their health leave or their obstetrician's golf commitments. Plastic surgeons remodel lined faces and sagging bodies as if rehabbing a bathroom. We can now project ourselves in image and voice all over the world at any time. We are ageless, 24/7 multipresent multitaskers, which is why some of us feel so distracted and overwhelmed and flee to the woods—to unplug and *re-member* our selves.

By late afternoon the dripping stops and I go outside to inspect the lump of granite. At first touch, I think I feel a small depression. But no, there is nothing, not the slightest indentation. I don't pick the rock up, or move it, but leave it exactly where it is, knowing it will rain again, and again, and again. My hope: in forty years, when my young son, Bennett, is my age, he will be sitting in this cabin someday and notice a steady dripping and then go outside to find the fist-sized rock. Then he will touch the tiny dent in eternity that bridges our lives and be filled with wonder.

Wonder, and the reverence it brings, is the best part of human nature. I feel it now—standing in the meadow amid the weeds and pine trees at dusk. Planted twenty-five years ago in what was then an old soybean field, these 30-foot-high white pines share the fading light and sandy clay with some red oaks and cottonwood. It is spring in southwest Michigan, so the foxtails and goldenrods are coming in. The bright trill of birdsong and the rumbling whir of Interstate 94, just a mile away, ride the same breeze. This evening, other than the unmistakable lament of a mourning dove, I recognize only two birdcalls: a cardinal and a robin. The rest of the dipping whistles and twittering vibratos are a blur. I blame this on the usual suspects—starlings, those great impersonators—rather than my ignorance. A good birder would know, could tell the difference between an imitation and the real thing. But I can't, and get lost somewhere in the middle.

So I try to compare the sounds of the birds to those of the distant engines—the melody of bone and blood against the drone of steel and diesel. The unending stream of semitrucks migrates north toward Holland, or east to Detroit, or back south toward Chicago. Yesterday, I walked the three-quarters of a mile from the cabin to I-94 and stood on the thundering overpass with my eyes closed for twenty minutes, listening intently. But I could not discern the different breeds. The Peterbilt, the Mack, and the Kenworth all sounded and smelled the same—the roar of approach, the slight quaver of the bridge, the smoky burn of retreat. These trucks haul huge transfer containers that were filled with shirts in the Philippines, or shoes in Indonesia, or telephones in China, or mangoes in Mexico. There are millions of them in perpetual migration. They carry whatever we want wherever we want it yet never quite relieve our longing, our hunger for something else, something unseen.

I return to the cabin, light a thick, red candle, and sit down with *Walden*. The next time I look up dusk has become night. Darkness consumes every tree and stone. The birds stop singing and the crickets start. Interstate 94, however, is relentless. Tomorrow night I will ride that river of headlights back to my home and family in suburban Chicago. On those two-hour trips around Lake Michigan through the darkness, I'm always aware of how *in between* I live: in between the woods and the mega mall, the blue jay and the Buick, the wild and the mundane, the animal and the human.

The more I wander around in *Walden,* the more I admire how Thoreau sees the wild *in* the mundane, the animal *in* the human, and the deep wonder in a life in the woods or anywhere else. Perhaps such insights were more common in preindustrial nineteenth-century America. But I doubt it. Thoreau also lived in between an imagined world of pure nature and an impure human-built world, though both were different from ours.

Even when he lived in town, there was no electricity or running water or indoor toilets or anything like what we now call health care. The leading cause of death for women was childbirth, and the second cause was fire, usually related to cooking. Tuberculosis was widespread and claimed Thoreau's life when he was only forty-four. His beloved brother, John, died from tetanus at twenty-six. Penobscot Indians still wandered into town from time to time to sell baskets. The telegraph had just been invented. And the railroad, cutting-edge technology, had newly arrived in Concord, passing just five hundred feet from Thoreau's cabin.

The candle flame jumps in a gust of wind, almost expires. Then a coyote starts to howl—maybe two. I rarely hear them. They sound close. Where exactly are they? I open the screen door, take a few steps out, and shine a flashlight randomly into the darkness, the beam bouncing around the meadow like a police searchlight, revealing only weeds. It has no effect on the coyotes. But soon the staggered "Yawooo, ooo-woowoo" changes, begins to sound less threatening than mournful.

When I sit back down, my laptop beeps and blinks a "critical" message—only a 4 percent charge left in the battery. I follow the computer's advice and save my work on the hard drive. Then the screen fades to black, and I'm left with the flickering candle. In the shadowy, uneven light, I find myself wondering what it was like here in Sawyer during Thoreau's life. I know that the town was named for a German immigrant, Silas Sawyer. He cleared forty acres of woods nearby and planted an apple orchard in 1854, the same year *Walden* was published. The next year, he built a steam sawmill near the lake and the Chicago and Western Railroad built a station, naming the settlement after the pioneer.

Today, Sawyer is the same size as Concord was in the mid-nineteenth century—about two thousand people. And the cabin we built is a mile and a half away from the town center—about the same distance between Thoreau's cabin and downtown Concord. Even now, as I write, I can hear the train whistle in Sawyer. But given the radical evolution in travel from train to plane, the whistle no longer marks the inevitability of westward expansion. Rather, it is a romantic, comforting sound from yesteryear. It carries for me the same nostalgia that the clip-clop of a horse did for my parents in their rural childhood, when Model As and Ts began to replace the horse-drawn buggy.

Progress: the constant redefinition of *fast* and *convenient*. This often concerns Thoreau in *Walden*. But he is less worried about new technology than what it will do to human experience. He sees the old form of transportation, the horse, within the new one, the train: "The iron horse makes the hills echo with his snort like thunder, shaking the earth with his feet."[2] Yet he is leery of the unbridled engine: "We do not ride on the railroad; it rides upon us."[3]

The fat, red candle on the table has burnt a well in its heart, which has filled with molten wax and drowned the flame. I don't relight it. It is darker in the cabin than outside. The moon is full and bathes the trees in a light so soft and clean, it feels dreamt. The glowing rays of light reach for the earth and turn everything they touch—even the rocks and weeds—into something holy. I spread my sleeping bag on the floor and lie near a window where I can ponder the radiant eye of the moon.

Maybe it's because the moon is watching me, or because the coyotes' howls and yips seem too loud and too close. Or maybe I'm just lonely and miss my family. But for whatever reason, I can't sleep. I get up, pour the hot puddle of red candle wax into an empty jar, straighten the wick, light it, and pull out a Xeroxed article from a thick manila folder in my backpack. It is labeled "Human/Nature."

I read the article—a new study from the University of Illinois that confirms the human bewilderment I have been thinking about all day: people don't know how, if, or why they belong to the "natural world," or even what the natural world is.[4]

Those in the study were first asked to define *nature* and *unnatural,* and then to define themselves as natural or unnatural—as part of nature, or separate. Three-quarters of the participants considered themselves "part of nature." But when asked to define *nature,* two-thirds of the same group said it was a place "undisturbed by humans," places that "don't include humans or human-made entities." And when asked to write words that described "unnatural" environments, most of the responses involved human-made elements: suburbs, cities, concrete, electric and phone wires, factories and pollution. Most Americans understand nature or wilderness as a place where people aren't.

But this is not a new insight. The landmark Wilderness Act of 1964 defined *wilderness* as an area "untrammeled by man." This legislation was meant to protect the natural world from people, even though we *are* animals, descendants of ever more primitive primates and other creatures. The problem is we don't act like we're related, like we belong to something bigger. And very few technological advances since Thoreau's time have helped restore that belonging.

Still wide awake, I stick the article back in the folder and dig out my own journal—some lighter reading. My rambling, disjointed record of the past sometimes calms me in the present. I ruffle through it and read here and there before stopping at an entry that is a few years old, back when handheld computers were still a novelty.

JULY 24
Carol and I and the kids had a good day at the lake. It was hot—mid-nineties—the cool water felt great. Something odd though: amid the blazing heat, a young guy was sitting near us on a towel in the sand—working on a little handheld computer. He was typing madly with his thumbs. I asked him what he was doing. "Just staying in touch with the office," he said. "I love my BlackBerry." This made no sense to me.

I knew about BlackBerrys, but I'd never used one or seen one up close. And I was puzzled as to why the little blinking, beeping plastic brain was named after my favorite fruit. Blackberry canes thrive in the sandy soil around our cabin, amid the sunny patches of meadow on the edge of the woods. So what was the connection between this lovely fruit and this expensive high-tech device? What was "natural" about it?

Nothing, of course. And everything. I did some research: the BlackBerry's designers had noticed that the little buttons looked like the tiny seeds of a strawberry. But they thought "straw" sounded too slow to represent the speed and 24/7 ultraconvenience of the modern business world. Thus, because it was black, they decided on "BlackBerry." The naming of the BlackBerry was a marketing strategy. Big surprise. Everything I buy in the grocery store, from tea to toothpaste to toilet paper, has "All Natural" stamped on it. Nature sells.

Even so, I'm still tempted by the BlackBerry. My problem is that I both fear and need one. I need one to help get organized and caught up. Like most people, my life sometimes slips into sprawl mode—unchecked growth in too many directions: work, marriage, three kids in three schools, committees, church, friends, neighbors, and on and on. I don't handle this well. The e-mails and texts telling me where to be and what to do and how to vote sometimes pile up into a mountain of information I don't know how to climb. I'm not sure why. Maybe because nowhere in all those thousands of words is the gentle anchor of the human voice.

As the technology gets smarter and faster, I get dumber and slower, and more distracted. This became clear to me last week when I again lost my car in the college parking lot. After a ten-minute search in the rain on the acre of blacktop, I finally found it. I pretended that I knew where I was going, but it was embarrassing. And last month, I found my billfold in the cheese drawer of the refrigerator after I finally decided to stop looking for it and finish making my lunch. And more than once I've been surprised at a stop sign, when a ceramic mug of hot coffee comes flying off the roof of my car, bounces off the hood, and shatters on the street.

Perhaps these are all signs of something ominous, or of something increasingly common: living between the past and the future, but never quite in the present.

All of which is why I fear getting a BlackBerry. I worry that I'll save so much time that I won't waste any. I'll be so damned programmed and productive that I'll never go a-fishing in Thoreau's stream of wonder, or do anything that matters. Like pick real blackberries with the kids, or write, which are two of my favorite things to do. And I enjoy them for the same reason: both are a kind of searching and gathering. It all has to do with memory, with remembering the slow weave of my life with my children's in this place. But I can't program that into a computer.

Searching and gathering. Remembering. I put my laptop back in its case, snuff the candle, lie back down, close my eyes, and think of blackberries. I picked them in these Michigan woods with my parents and brothers forty years ago. And now Carol and I do the same with our kids. Little has changed. The berries still ripen in August, marking the end of summer and of the wild, unmeasured hours of childhood. The thorns still scratch and cut us as we reach into the thicket for the ripe, black clusters. The purple juice still bleeds onto our hands and stains them.

I taste it now, the aching sweet and sour of a ripe blackberry, even as I lie here and listen to the high chirping tremolo of the crickets' thin, dark wings and the low, barreling wane of the semis roaring into the night. Somehow they all converge in the darkness, with a drip of rain on a fist of stone as the timeless rhythm of creation, the tender music of our belonging.

Chapter 2

In Plain Sight
Vision and Revision

Let the seer bring down his broad eye to
the most stale and trivial fact, and he will
make you believe it a new planet in the sky.

HENRY DAVID THOREAU, *Journal*[1]

Darkness. But dawn is near. So those of us who don't see or feed or travel well at night, but only sleep and dream, can rise again into the comforting mystery of light. The sun wheels over the horizon—opens flowers and lifts insects into their wild buzzing stop-and-go lives. It makes the trees glow, the weeds sparkle, and the barn swallows whistle for their mates. But when it clears the tops of the white pines, it is in my eyes and I can't read the computer screen. I move my chair and laptop to a shadowed corner of the cabin, where I stare at the woods, sip bitter day-old coffee, and wait for words. But none come, so I walk outside.

A great blue heron pumps slowly across the empty sky. He is headed toward the small river that marks the eastern boundary of our land. Last month five pairs of herons flapped back to our farm, as they have for the past three years, to repair their great prickly bowls of sticks and lay their eggs. The nests are about three feet across and set near the top of a ninety-foot-high sycamore tree. It drapes over the Galien River, which is twenty-five miles long and snakes all over Berrien County before draining into Lake Michigan. Thirty years ago, the Galien was loaded with fish and was a favorite swimming hole for those who didn't live on the lake. But today it's very sick. Last year, the Michigan Department of Environmental Quality declared it "unsafe for even partial bodily contact." A sample taken at a bridge just down the road contained forty times the acceptable level of E. coli bacteria.

Though herons are not endangered, and rookeries with dozens of nests and hundreds of birds are common, the return of these birds to our farm gives me hope. And the hope is deeper this year, as I can now count seven new nests in an even taller sycamore on the other side of the river. These birds may be the offspring of the first year's hatching, as herons often return to their parents' nesting site two or three years later. I'm not sure whether the herons thrive here because of the new conservation program to clean up the river and control soil erosion, or simply because they know how to adapt. Either way, if they can find enough fish and frogs to feed themselves and their offspring, it's a good sign.

Agriculture, unfettered industry, and new development have poisoned this land, as they have much of the Midwest. So the animals that live here are the tough kind—raccoons, possums, and coyotes, starlings, grackles, and turkey vultures—species that quickly adapted to the damaged habitat, to the half-million-dollar vacation homes that have started popping up just down the road, to erosion and fertilizers and pesticides and herbicides, and to the river, which has absorbed these toxins. These same animals are considered pests in Glen Ellyn, the Chicago suburb where we live. But who can blame them for excelling at adaptation and survival— a knack they share with people? Their abundance, and the rapid extinction of myriad other species, is mainly due to the human being—to our inability to belong to the ecosystem, to imagine "enough" of anything.

Evidence of this human never-enoughness is everywhere. The E. coli bacteria level in our river is one good example. Much of it comes from human waste, from broken and leaking septic systems.[2] Though it also comes from raising cattle not on their natural diet of grass but on corn, which screws up their digestive tracts. It's too much starch for them and creates a dangerous strain of bacteria (0157:H7), which also pollutes nearby rivers. The reason for corn feeding is economic: corn-fed cattle reach slaughter weight in a little over a year, while grass-fed cattle require four to five years. Cattle farmers accelerate this process with growth hormones and must also use antibiotics to offset the harmful effects of corn on the cows' intestines. These chemicals all find their way into the woodland stream, and ultimately into the human bloodstream.

Last week I read a little piece of this chapter to my teenage daughter, Tessa. I was preparing an excerpt for a radio essay about the herons and wanted to see what she thought. She stopped me when I said the word *polluted* because it didn't align with what she had seen.

"The river's polluted?" she asked. "But I think it's beautiful."

"I do too," I said. "It's just that there's a lot we can't see: chemical runoff, farm waste, leaking septic tanks. That kills a lot of plants and fish."

"Oh," she said in a tone that means, "That's enough. I'm going to tune out now."

Like Tessa, my eyes are not scientifically trained to see very far past the Galien's facade of health. But on my frequent walks, I notice that minnows and panfish are very rare. I've seen no crawdads backing out of their mud holes along the riverbank and no turtles sunning themselves on deadfall trees. Tadpoles and frogs should be still more abundant. And I presume that all the algae growth diminishes oxygen levels. Yet a recent state Department of Natural Resources and Environment report verified trout and walleye in a part of the river that is less polluted and closer to the lake. As I watch the slow-moving water, I wonder if those fish will ever live here, in this neck of the Galien. I would be happy just to see a sucker or a carp—the bottom feeders I loved to catch as a kid.

I walk along the river carrying both the burden of my role in its slow destruction and the hope of the returning herons. I'm not sure how a writer can resolve such conflicts, though it matters *how* we write about nature. Broadly speaking, it seems some nature writers primarily seek to discover the unspoiled, exotic bits of wilderness, which they fly to in jets and bush planes. Other writers seek more to recover the spoiled, the nonwilderness. They observe and analyze and reflect on their own towns and cities and suburbs and backyards. There is value in both approaches, and they sometimes blur or overlap, but I most identify with those writers who stay put, who know their own ground. And the truth is, I don't really have a choice: no magazine has offered to fly me to the highlands of Guatemala to count quetzals or to the Aleutian Islands to track migrating whales.

Yet, clearly the reason the "untouched" wilderness has become increasingly polluted is because it *has* been touched. Exploration of the Arctic, of coral reefs, and of rain forests has invariably led to exploitation, and to dozens of ecological disasters. Sadly, the most catastrophic of these is recent: the British Petroleum oil spill in the Gulf of Mexico last year. And things are not getting better. Which is why, instead of trying to get to some new or "pure" bit of the natural world, we need to also seek the Wild in the restoration of ruin—in something so humdrum as the return of "rough" fish and fowl and wildflowers to the devastated forests and rivers of the Midwest.

I would like to start now—not with the marvel of the untouched, but with learning how to be touched by the commonplace, on this piece of land we call "the farm." What most interests me here is the natural miracle of revision, of learning to see again. I am looking less for a pure subject than for a moment of pure vision: to see what is in plain sight—a glimpse of the Wild in the ordinary. Wildness, as Thoreau demonstrates over and over, is not an undiscovered insect or island, but a quality of awareness, a way of seeing. "To an adventurous spirit," he writes, "any place—London, New York, Worcester, is unexplored land . . . . To a sluggish and defeated spirit, even the Great Basin and Polaris are trivial places."[3]

It hasn't rained for ten days, so the river is only 3 feet deep, and quite clear. When I reach the next bend and look south, I see the beauty Tessa does: the stony riffles and gurgles around rocks and deadfalls and an abandoned tractor tire. A timeless current runs along the yellow sandy bottom as the shimmering surface flickers sunlight back at the wildflowers. The delicate yellow wheels and purple cups and white-petaled tubes—spring beauties, phlox, trillium, jack-in-the-pulpit—dot the green explosion of returning foliage. The trees have already turned the sunlight into a half-formed canopy, which will keep closing for several more weeks until it blocks most of the light and wind from the woods. By then the herons will no longer be visible, and the mosquitoes will be breeding and rising in swarms off the river into the humming, blood-seeking clouds that drift through the stillness and shadow, looking for me.

The other blood seekers I know best—the deer ticks and dog ticks—are already out, though not in full force. They sit waiting for our warm mammalian blood—in trees and on vines and on the tips of tall grasses, always ready to attack, or to *attach* to, whatever deer or dog or raccoon or person they can find. This behavior, this perching on the leaves and stems with forelegs extended, is called questing. When something brushes them, they climb on and plunge a beaklike projection into the warm flesh, drawing in a quantity of blood that is a hundred times their "empty" weight. It is mostly the dog ticks that find me—the bigger ones. They crawl out of my socks, or I feel them creeping on my ankles or down my back. I end their quest as quickly as I can, not wanting to find a bloated tick in the morning.

I keep walking along the river. Fifty yards ahead, a thin four-foot-high gray-feathered statue stands in the river's swampy oxbow. The curve of the bird's thin neck, head, and beak, and the straight of his body, form a ruffled question mark. Presuming he is fishing, I also freeze. This is only the second time I've seen a heron on the ground and not scared it away. Because of the sentinel warning system they use around the rookery, it's hard to get close to one. I watch him for several minutes, but he soon lifts off in a wild thwapping, unfolding seven feet of wing.

Though I've never seen a heron catch a fish on the Galien, I have watched them eat small sunfish at a lake near our home in Glen Ellyn, tilting back their heads to gurgle-swallow them whole. They spear the fish as near the head as possible to wound or kill them before eating them. Audubon once wrote about watching a heron try to spear a fish in Florida that was so big that the heron's beak got stuck. The fish pulled the impaler under the water and nearly drowned it before the bird could unhook itself and escape from its prey.

I keep trudging along the river through the wild rose brambles and reeds. Soon I can hear the herons' odd, grumbling conversation in their nests in the distance. They sound like my Uncle Carl—rough, low voices—like they're trying to both clear their throat and tease me with a question. "Whaht? Whaht? Whaht? Whaht are you doing?" is what I hear.

"I'm watching," I say aloud. "Just watching." I visit the birds only every three or four weeks, as I don't want to disturb them. Sometimes, heron fledglings become so flustered by predators or other distractions that they fall out of their nest and die only days before learning to fly.

When I arrive at the old sycamore, I lie flat on my back underneath it with my binoculars aimed at the nests. I keep watching until I feel a warm, sticky dripping on my arm—and then on my neck. Could it be . . . ? Yes, it is: guano rain. The birds are shitting on me. I wonder whether it's intentional, whether I am a target.

I take the hint, but just before I leave, one bird gets anxious.

She peers over the rim of the nest at me with a haunting yellow-ringed eye, makes her decision, nervously stumbles around in the sticks for a second, unfolds that great prehistoric S of a body, and tumbles into the air with an awkward beauty, quickly drop-gliding to the river bank. Surprised she has flown down rather than up, I remain still and watch the odd stalk of bone and feather and beak take three slow, methodical steps along the sandy bank before pivoting her head to look at me. She is harried, but unlike a sparrow or wren, not equipped for quick, fluid movements.

The gawky lifting of her body from the river reminds me of one of the Wright brothers' early flying machines, which you were never quite sure would make it through takeoff. But unlike those early planes, the heron becomes more graceful as she rises over the water. Once aloft, she is easy in the air. She flies across the canvas of the day as she has for a thousand years, stroking the empty sky with the wild brush of her gray-blue wings. As I watch her circle our land, this plot of nonwilderness, I wonder what she sees. I wonder what she, and the trees, and the river know about the fragile strands of the trembling web that is holding us together.

Chapter 3

Fathers Watching Sons

Windows and Mirrors

Children, who play life, discern its true law and relations more clearly than men, who fail to live it worthily, but who think they are wiser by experience, that is, by failure.

HENRY DAVID THOREAU, *Walden*[1]

Drip. Drip. Drip. A familiar sound. Today it's not rain on stone, but a leaky kitchen faucet. I wish I knew how to replace the cracked gasket, but I don't. We have been waiting for weeks for a second plumbing problem that would warrant the plumber's $100 minimum fee for a visit. The monotony of the constant drip is driving me nuts. I put a folded towel under it at night, but I can still hear it—even upstairs in bed. Carol says I'm imagining it, but I don't think so.

I had planned to go to the cabin today for two days of writing, but Bennett has a fever and can't go to school. And Carol has an all-day conference. So I'm working on the laptop in the family room and listening to the drip, while Bennett plays on the floor at my feet. In spite of his illness, he is happily lost amid a couple of gallons of Legos and has no sense of how slowly time is passing. Nor does he hear the dripping faucet. We just found the Legos at a garage sale, and their newness, the infinite possibilities, enthrall him. He sits rapt on the carpet inventing and quietly talking to himself—as if conferring with another seven-year-old inventor.

Every fifteen minutes or so, after he has clicked a few more of the red, blue, and green plastic pieces together, he shows me something.

"Look, Daddy. See this guy? He's driving the ship." Then a bit later: "Look, Daddy, I put a coffee maker on the main ship. But I put a lemonade maker on the shuttle."

"Which is the shuttle?" I ask, now understanding it is a rocket ship, rather than a sailing ship.

"Here. Look!" he says, unhitching a red matchbox-size platform from the main ship. A driver sits in a little chair, and I assume a green thimble-size cylinder attached to the back is the lemonade maker. He flies the shuttle completely around the sofa, making a whooshing noise all the while and pausing twice to fire imaginary machine guns at a couple of Hot Wheels cars below him. Then he lands it on my thigh. There he takes the driver out, straightens his legs, and walks him to my knee, which is now clearly a precipice looking out on an alternate universe. An inch tall, the plastic, square-headed man surveys the messy terrain of the family room.

"He's an explorer," Bennett says.

"What kind of explorer?" I ask.

"I don't know. Like a Power Ranger, or maybe an Indian."

Well, I wasn't expecting Meriwether Lewis, but the odd contrast of cultures fascinates me, as does the power of Bennett's raw imagination—all that he sees and discovers in a pile of discarded plastic Legos. *He* is the explorer who most impresses me.

Last week he brought me a red truck to repair. He broke off its wheels while "driving" (bouncing) it down the stairs and then left it on my workbench in the basement. The cracked wheels were plastic and couldn't be glued or replaced—a lost cause. Or so I thought.

"That's OK. I'll keep it, Daddy," Bennett said as he carried it back upstairs to the playroom. I see it now on the carpet—a red plastic sled hitched up to a three-legged horse with a Star Wars character riding in the flatbed. Luke Skywalker seems to be lashing the horse with his lightsaber. I'm still not sure why the horse is standing upright despite its disability, or how Bennett knew that it would. I just don't see that way.

This feeling, this inability to see, is not new. I used to get it each day when I dropped Bennett off at the preschool at the college where I teach. Because it was a lab school, there was a long one-way teaching mirror in the front hallway. Students and parents could look in at the kids without them seeing us—our window was their mirror. But it took me several days to even notice this. I was often in a hurry. After the sign-in sheet, the hug, the nod to his teacher, I usually bolted off to my office with my briefcase to do important things.

Yet one day, on the way out, I paused for a moment and caught a glimpse of my distracted self in the window. That's not the way it's supposed to work. The kids are supposed to see themselves on the other side. But when I took two steps toward my faint, self-absorbed reflection, it disappeared. My "I" yielded to my eye, which suddenly saw through to the world on the other side, the world I so often just walked by: children sprawled everywhere on the carpet in a kind of wild and holy innocence—working wooden puzzles, reading board books, rocking dolls, singing silly songs. My God, they were delirious with curiosity, and I was thrown into their childhood, and my own, so abruptly that I found myself in tears.

What was it about this window?

I could see the kids, but they couldn't see me. If they tried to look back at me, all they saw was themselves and their own world: four-year-old Maggie, in glittery pink slippers and a baggy green velvet dress and two strings of white plastic pearls, stirred a pan of air on a little wooden stove with a rubber spatula and intently adjusted the dials until the temperature was just right. Then James came running over with a little snake he had rolled from a ball of blue Play-Doh and popped it in Maggie's pan. This perturbed her at first, but soon she began to stir it in and to readjust the dials. Bennett, who wore a black-and-silver stethoscope, sat cross-legged on the carpet next to Maggie and diligently checked the heart rate of the stuffed green dinosaur he was cradling. Then he tucked it into to a wooden crib and whispered something to it—perhaps a bedtime prayer.

How odd it was to see Bennett but not be seen by him, to be in the same room with him, yet not. When I got up to leave for the office, and was several feet away from the window, I again turned it into a mirror, again caught my dim likeness in the glass. It was then that I finally saw the obvious: I was watching Bennett through the dim reflection of myself, weighing my own childhood against his, the known against the unknown. That's a hard thing for parents—to stop seeing ourselves in our children. And to stop waiting—consciously or not—for them to demonstrate that one attribute or flaw that marks them as a part of us. As they get older, I wonder who will be blessed with a modicum of musical or athletic ability, and who might inherit my impatience or depression.

But thankfully, the dimming mirror is also a sparkling-clear window.

And I think that paradox was the source of my tears and confusion that day at the lab school. I saw myself in the presence of those little kids and wanted to crawl on all fours back into their world, to dress myself up in their total surrender to the *now,* and in a kind of vision that could turn Legos into spaceships and Play-Doh into edible blue snakes. When, I wonder, did I first begin to lose my faith in the moment I was living in? When did my life first start to feel like a faucet that never stops dripping, like a sprawling to-do list?

২৯

Like me, my own dad sometimes struggled to see life's blessings amid its burdens, and to shift from the I to the eye, from self to world. He too could get overwhelmed by work, and the future, and struggle to get back to the present. Or at least that's how it seems now, in the shadows of memory. But that was all a long time ago. Dad and Mom are close to ninety now. And though they have sharp minds and still swim most days, their bodies are wearing down as they approach the deepest mystery of all.

Yet it was just forty years ago that Dad was my age and I was a little kid. And he sometimes picked me up at the lab school in Ames, Iowa, where he was a young pastor with a large church and four sons. I can see him leaning on the chain-link fence on the edge of the preschool playground, watching me play freeze tag on the blacktop with my four-year-old friends. And there, I imagine him, in his sport coat and slacks, waiting and watching us for a few slow minutes before calling my name, before waving me in— before hugging me, zipping up my open coat, adjusting my hat, and taking me home. Just a minute or two of pause, of revision, before returning to *real* time.

Maybe it's because I'm now almost exactly between my son and my father—forty years older than Bennett and forty years younger than my dad—that these small moments seem sacred. This morning I'm wondering how my dad found such moments along the way—amid the chaos of family and church, amid all those sermons and meetings and potlucks. But I'm hoping he did sometimes, while lingering on the edge of that playground. Hoping that my little friends and I, in our crazy games of tag and kickball, could—like Bennett did for me—somehow loosen the grip of time, giving him a moment of presence, of prayer.

⁂

By midmorning Bennett is still lost in his Legos. I tell him I'm going into the kitchen to clean the floor. He says, "OK," but after about ten minutes, he calls in to me, "Where'd you go, Daddy?"

"I'm in the kitchen," I say.

"OK," he says, again seemingly satisfied. A few minutes later, he carries in an armload of Lego spaceships and shuttles and sets up shop on the kitchen table. Soon, he is sailing off to other galaxies and planets while I scrub the floor on all fours. It is not long before he flies one of his Lego ships over my head and dramatically ejects the pilot into my pail with a soapy *kerplunk!* and a squeal of laughter.

"He can't swim! He can't swim!" I say. Bennett laughs.

The rest of the morning seems to pass quickly, or I barely notice that it's passing. Bennett keeps drawing me back into his play, and then I return to cleaning. I know this is called parallel play, and that I should be fully engaged with him rather than trying to finish my work projects. But this is the best I can do today. And he seems pretty happy. Later, when I get out a sleeve of Ritz crackers and a can of 7-Up, he looks both excited and thankful for the simple snack.

"I like staying home with you, Daddy," he says as he starts to make lean-tos and little towers out of the crackers.

"Yeah, I like it too," I say.

⁂

That night, after everyone is in bed, I sit up, as I have for the last few months, and read a few pages of *Walden*. I escape for twenty minutes into Thoreau's isolated life at the pond in search of words that might still inspire:

> We should be blessed if we lived in the present always, and took advantage of every accident that befell us, like the grass which confesses the influence of the slightest dew that falls on it; and did not spend our time in atoning for the neglect of past opportunities, which we call doing our duty.[2]

Translation: *be here now.*

Though Thoreau may have lacked the "dutiful" patience or practicality to be a father himself, he had a rare childlike wonder I often envy—a lost-in-the-Legos presence. He tried to live in what he called "the gospel of this moment," seemingly unfettered to anything but the sun and the woods and the pond. I can't imagine him ever writing out a to-do list. Maybe a to-be list? And what would he put on that? Maybe "Awestruck" or "Amazed" or "Bedazzled"?

These words get me thinking about Bennett again, and a question he asked tonight at bedtime—out of the blue:

"How did somebody know that there was a carrot growing beneath the leaves on top? How did they know it wasn't just a regular root? Who figured that out?"

"Do you mean, who discovered the carrot?" I asked.

"Yeah, I guess."

"I don't really know. But I know that the Indians and other people who lived before they had electricity and grocery stores had to figure out what to eat in order to survive. So they ate animals that they killed, and experimented with all kinds of plants and roots as food."

"But how did they know the first time that carrots would taste good?"

"They probably didn't. They probably just tasted them. Maybe they had eaten other roots and the smell and color and snap of the carrot root told them these were good ones too." I was just getting warmed up, just about to tell him all that I knew about carrots as a staple food in Africa and Asia—

"OK," Bennett said, meaning that this answer was enough and he didn't need any more info. Satisfied, and tired, he reached over, flicked off his lamp, and then said what I usually say: "Lights out."

I smiled, tucked him in, and walked down the hall to our bedroom, thankful for the moment, for all of these moments.

Chapter 4

Saunter

Reason and Instinct

The Saunterer . . . is no more vagrant than the meandering river, which is all the while sedulously seeking the shortest course to the sea.

HENRY DAVID THOREAU[1]

A week later, I drive back to the cabin for a couple of days. I wake early and decide to walk the boundary trail, which follows our land's periphery. Before leaving, I dig out and drop on the table a wad of twenty jangling gold and silver keys—to two cars, the farmhouse, my office, the shed, the garage, the cabin, the bike locks, the copy room, and who knows what else. Then I pull out a billfold bulging with plastic: Visa and MasterCard, ATM and phone and gift and health insurance cards, licenses and photo IDs. The cash slot is stuffed with receipts and coupons and blank checks, four one-dollar bills, and an individually wrapped Earl Grey tea bag.

Why is this small act, this emptying, so satisfying? And why do I sometimes carry my keys and billfold when I go walking in the woods? Do I imagine I'll find a hidden lockbox in the buggy tangle, or a new cash station in the beaver dam near the oxbow?

I walk out of the cabin, cross the creek, and soon reach the meadow, where I'm lured by the warm sun to sit in the grass. I notice a dimple in the ground behind me, about the size and depth of a plum split in half. With my eyes a few inches away, I can see a sparkling prism of sticky dew beads: a sheet web (which, if actually a sheet, would bed down only a small grasshopper). A spider with a head and body like two saffron grains of sand waits on the rainbow of light it has built, listening for prey with all eight legs. Two black ants walking in different directions over the lovely trap on the stable bridge of a green blade of grass have just enough room to pass without pushing the other off.

Since the ants don't stop to investigate with their antennae (parts of which serve as both their noses and fingertips), they seem oblivious to the potential peril that looms below them. Ah, the tiny life of the tiny ant: no anxiety, or ignorance, or heroism—just food and reproduction and the chemicals that drive them toward it. How much simpler can a life get? And how much more meaningless? There are no saunters, just the march toward survival. My guess is that the ants would take their keys and billfolds if they could.

I follow the circuitous route of one of the ants for several minutes on all fours. Just when I tire of tracking him, I hear it: a slight yet constant clicking noise—the sounds of thousands of ant legs tapping the brittle, dry leaves as they walk—like a light, tender rain.

Suddenly ants are everywhere, all moving toward the sandy hill I now notice a few feet away. There are seventy or eighty entry holes leading inside a mound about the size of my head. Little crews of four or five workers are bringing all kinds of things home for their queen—a piece of a june bug's wing, fragments of grass and leaf and lichen. But the biggest prize is a large iridescent green housefly, perfectly preserved. None of its legs or wings have yet been bitten off. The eight ants that are carrying the fly are mobbed when they reach the top of the hill, buried by a frenetic swarm of kicking legs. The fly disappears under the writhing mound of ants and then reemerges on the backs of a half-dozen different ants that quickly move it to one of the entry holes and try to push it through. They pull the thorax in, but the head gets stuck. The mob returns, and another cadre pulls out the green carcass and tries to jam it down a different hole. The fifth attempt is successful: the hole is big enough, and the fly disappears into the inner world of the hill. I'm relieved. The scene reminds me of a news clip I saw last year while teaching in England: a hooligan riot at a soccer game in Manchester—a chaotic mob of drunks piling in the bleachers, each lost in the sprawl, in some primal instinct to come out on top.

Ants are also intensely aggressive: ant wars over territory or food result in both sides literally ripping each other to pieces, the killing field a repository of twitching legs. A popular story in *Walden*, "The Battle of the Ants," describes such a scene. After watching for a while, Thoreau removes a woodchip from the ant battleground, on which an isolated struggle continues. He takes the chip with the warring red and black ants into his cabin and puts it under a glass tumbler. Using the glass as a crude microscope, he describes how the red ant's "breast was all torn away, exposing what vitals he had there to the jaws of the black warrior." He then sympathizes with the "loser": "[T]he dark carbuncles of the sufferer's eyes shone with ferocity such as war only could excite."[2]

Thoreau's emotional personification of the soldier ant is laid against a broader analogy—his critique of the Mexican War and the American Revolutionary War and the futility of war in general. The allegory is overt. While watching the ant battle, Thoreau comments, "I was myself excited somewhat even as if they had been men. The more you think of it, the less the difference."[3]

But since Thoreau's time, entomologists have discovered much more about those differences. Unlike those English hooligans in Manchester, ants struggle less to come out on top than to just keep coming out. Ants are relentless and resilient, and their fecundity and dominance are due to their altruism, to each ant's selfless performance of a given duty. This cooperative behavior evolved over a hundred million years ago as a means of strengthening defenses against enemies and finding more food. It has been quite successful. Today there are more than a million ants for each person on the planet. And the total weight of all those ants equals the total weight of all the people.

"The great strength of ants," writes E. O. Wilson, "is their ability to create tight bonds and complex social arrangements with tiny brains."[4] Their "thought" is not individualized but collective. The interdependence of their world inside the hill is remarkable—particularly in reproduction: the adult ants nurture the eggs and pupae and larvae by licking them, which keeps them from getting moldy. When I first learned this in a college biology class, I wanted to personify, to believe it was a sign of affection, that the ants *loved*. But of course it's not, and they don't: the eggs and larvae are covered with a sweet liquid that attracts the adults. They feed the larvae for the same reason. When an adult puts food in its mouth, a sweet liquid is secreted as a reward.

In a biology lab, we filled a petri dish with water and then made a little island of sand in the middle. We put red ant pupae on the island and then set the petri dish a few inches from a mound of sand that contained a colony of red ants. The point was to see whether the ants' nurturing instinct would cause them to build a bridge of sand to the abandoned pupae. Sure enough, they immediately started carrying and dumping sand and dirt particles into the water until a bridge was formed and they could reach the stranded pupae.

Then the teacher had us do the same experiment without the pupae. And of course the colony of ants did the same thing: they built a bridge to the island even though there were no pupae to rescue. Ants always throw sand or dirt in the water as an instinctive survival response to their hill or colony flooding. But the point of the two-part experiment was to remind us that science is subjective and that *research* is literally that—an unending process of searching. The experimenter "arrives" not at some final answer, but at a deeper set of questions. There is always a bit further to go.

In one way, the speck of an ant's brain seems disappointing, or absurd—the utter absence of choice, of love and passion. Yet as I watch the intricate complexity of the anthill—witness the ants laying down chemical trails to a food source, or their "mouth-to-mouth" passing of regurgitated food samples to one another—it strikes me that humans could never achieve such communal efficiency and economy. And that we too are absurdly trapped by our design, by the labyrinth of language and reason. We drown in choices, in possibilities, and in self-consciousness—so much so that even emptying one's pockets or watching a hill of ants can feel like an epiphany.

I get up and walk out of the meadow and into the woods. A cool, heavy mist hangs along the muddy bank of the river's oxbow. Wildflowers are everywhere: purple phlox and yellow swamp lilies startle against the gray-green trees and muddy brown leaf bed. The stark white of three blooming dogwoods above me and the trillium below me look as if some god had drenched a huge brush in pure white paint and given it a shake here and there in the woods.

Even the most common birds are spectacular in the dripping dew: A hopping robin is aflame on the trail ahead of me. A goldfinch lights on a maple sapling in front of the dark mass of a huge cottonwood trunk. The raw yellow against the wet blackness distracts me from the rush of a plane overhead, and from the high-pitched binding of a circular saw somewhere beyond the trees.

Along the river, I find the stretch of trail that will soon disappear in the thicket of the summer understory. Last July, I was wading through that overgrowth, feeling a bit unsure, looked down, and suddenly it was gone. I didn't know whether I was on the trail or was making my own. I couldn't see it. And then, finally, I did—an opening trodden in the weeds. Yet it was not as if I was ever really lost. I knew where the river and the farmhouse were, but it still startled me how quickly the trail disappeared, how I could be looking right at it and not see it.

A neighbor's dog on the other side of the river starts to howl—loud and crazed, as if it is on a chain and has seen a rabbit. I think of an odd little essay I taught in my composition classes last week: "Looking for a Lost Dog," by Gretel Ehrlich—a story about walking. Ehrlich starts off with a clear purpose—to find her dog, which is lost in the Wyoming wilderness. But after a few paragraphs, it is clear that she has lost her way, and is searching for the much deeper wilderness of her *self*. She is torn open by her desires: "Some days I think this one place isn't enough," she writes. "I want to live multiple lives and be allowed to love without limits." But the more she notices and attends to her environment, the more she is able to see, the more at home she becomes, until she finally recognizes that "everything is here." She closes with this line: "Today it is enough to make a shadow."

"But what the hell's her point?" asks Bill, a bright and witty student. "She makes me feel like *I'm* lost in the woods!"

Maybe, I say, that's her point: *we are all lost in the woods*—in the bramble of human limitation and longing. And thus we neither notice nor appreciate our ability to "make a shadow," the beauty of our simple presence, our human *being*.

"Why doesn't she just say that then?" Bill continues.

Maybe she wants us to participate in it, to feel it, I respond.

Bill looks pensive, and ready for class to end.

In the essay, Ehrlich also tips her hat to Thoreau, including this line from his essay "Walking": "The Saunterer is no more vagrant than the meandering river, which is all the while sedulously seeking the shortest course to the sea." Students often choose this as Ehrlich's thesis statement. Even though she didn't write it and they don't know what "sedulously" means (nor did I until I first read the essay), they sense that this simile is at the heart of things. Because it is a provocative sentence and we are learning basic research skills, I often ask students to paraphrase it. Here are a few responses from one class:

"The walker should not be faulted for taking his time."
"To saunter is more about being led than leading."
"The saunterer is not 'guilty,' nor is he lazy. He is wise."
"The walker knows where he is going, just as the river knows where it is going."

I like the last version—the idea that people and rivers both have the capacity to "know" important things, yet neither can understand the other's knowledge.

I walk through light and shadow, and then a dense quiet that is holding a word I can smell but not yet see. I think it is *death*. But perhaps it is *green*. The decaying floor of the woods, the dried blanket of brittle leaves and crumbling mash of log and stick, is perforated everywhere by green shoots, which are born to the light—maples and pawpaws and hickories and trout lilies and many more—all resurrected by the magnet of the sun. It is here, kneeling in the dank rot of the woods and watching the ants walking to and fro, that I can imagine the paradox of *arrival,* of ending as beginning, of the moment when the river enters the sea, when the current becomes part of a vast, deep stillness.

This image reminds me of some lines in one of Thoreau's letters I came across last week. He wrote it to console his friend, Ralph Waldo Emerson, just after the latter's five-year-old son, Waldo, had died of scarlet fever. Death is "a law and not an accident," Thoreau wrote. "It is as common as life. When we look over the fields we are not saddened because the particular flowers or grass will wither— for the law of their death is the law of new life. . . . So it is with the human plant."[5] Thoreau frequently addresses this idea in his work. "The human plant" flourishes as a part *of* nature but withers in seeking to be apart *from* nature. The sturdy white pine, and the sturdy young boy who climbs its sappy limbs, are always living and dying toward each other, and the Balance they create.

I walk up a steep hill, where I find my three favorite trees. The sycamore, beech, and cottonwood are all over a hundred feet tall. Their branches mingle in the sky, share leaping squirrels and nervous woodpeckers. Each tree has its own personality. The gray beech, with its tough, slick skin, is a dinosaur's neck bending and stretching to feed in the canopy. Its translucent leaves allow more light to pass through. Today the sun casts lime-tinted rays through the beech leaves onto the ground. The bark of the cottonwood conjures not skin but armor—a tough range of peaks and crevices so deep that Abby, my eleven-year-old daughter, can put her entire hand in one. The leaves of the cottonwood sapling are fat green hearts, with thick red veins, that so resemble an animal's circulatory system that they seem to pulsate with life. And the leaves' flat stems mean they cannot spin, but only bob from side to side in the wind, like they are constantly waving good-bye. The sycamore is the easiest to recognize of the trio, because it's always losing its skin. As it grows, the outer layer of bark can't keep pace and peels off into curling olive, white, and brown flakes. Thus it is typically dark on the lower half and bone white further up, where its molting is complete.

I most like to visit this elderly trio in the winter, when they are "dead" and the sap has run out of their hearts, and the core of their relationship, their competition for light and water, has all but stopped. Then I like to stand near them and listen to their creaking conversations as they scratch each other in the icy wind.

I keep walking. But I'm losing focus and starting to tire. I've stopped wandering and started wondering: How much further should I go? Should I not turn back, or at least point myself toward home? What time is it?

I sit on a rotten beech log to rest. The soft hollow of the tree is swarming with—what else?—thousands of ants. Their perfect chaos again pulls me into a trance. A long, black file marches across the soft wood like a sprawling prehistoric sentence. Each jointed body is an unpronounced letter, or an unspoken word, on its way to an idea hidden somewhere deep in the green mind of the woods. I follow the ants with my eyes until they hit their end mark, a dead sweat bee, where they heap up into a writhing mass of legs and mandibles.

This time, the stream of ants reminds me not of Thoreau's content but of his style, of how his long, winding sentences crawl into the soft tissue of the reader's brain, into mine, where the words pile into a wild throng of ideas. I am sometimes unsure whether Thoreau is exploring the language of nature or the nature of language. Probably both. Maybe this is why reading Thoreau always leads me back into the woods, back to walking.

Some days reading and walking seem like the same thing, like part of the same journey. Reading, too, is a kind of saunter, the sentences a faint path we track through the writer's consciousness. Some readers wander off in a direction the writer never imagined, following a faint, muddy paw print, or the warm ashes of a recent fire, toward some new idea or theme. Others get down on their hands and knees and savor the color and scent and flavor of certain words as if they were sacred. But many don't. Most of us want a clearly marked trail on which we can stop from time to time to briefly smell or touch or taste whatever is new, whatever momentarily startles or excites us. And then, like the ants, we need to get moving again, to march somewhere, to do something, to eat or have sex or change the oil, to try to arrive, and to avoid getting lost.

Maybe writers owe us this kind of clarity. Or maybe they don't. Maybe the point is that ants can't saunter, but people can, and so we should. Or maybe the point is that life is an ellipsis rather than a series of periods, that sauntering is all there really is, and the best sentences we will ever read or write or live only lead us deeper into the woods, into a place where keys and credit cards don't matter, a place where we once belonged, and still long to be.

Chapter 5

The Gay Cardinal
Love and Instinct

The Harivamsa says, "An abode without birds is like a meat without seasoning." Such was not my abode, for I found myself suddenly neighbor to birds; not by having imprisoned one, but having caged myself near them.

HENRY DAVID THOREAU, *Walden*[1]

This morning, Bennett and I are sitting out on the patio watching to see who visits our backyard bird feeder. It's just the regulars today—sparrows, grackles, finches, and a couple of chipmunks standing below in the rain of seed the birds kick out. Bennett has an old pair of binoculars and a journal to record the bird species he identifies. He has twenty or so now, but we just started a week ago. Like him, I don't know much about birds, but I love watching them, and sitting with him in the backyard, seeing what we can see in our little niche of the suburban wild.

Bennett's interest in birds was sparked last year when he first held one in his hands—a pine siskin. We were in Rocky Mountain National Park and had spent an afternoon with a naturalist, Jack, who showed us how to band birds to track their populations and migration patterns. Jack caught twenty-one birds from six species in two hours on nets he had strung near a couple of large feeders at the edge of the woods. After gently extracting the crossbill or nut-hatch or bluebird from the net, measuring the body and beak, and clipping the tiny metal bracelet onto the bird's leg, he often put the bird in the hand of one of the few children who were watching, so that they might return it to the wild.

I can't be sure, but I think Jack put the birds through this added thirty seconds of stress so the kids and their parents might "see" the birds, and Nature, in a deeper way. Feeling the warm pulse of blood within a living thing we hold in our hands doesn't just teach us about the Wild, it *includes* us in it. For a moment, we understand with our bodies that we and the bird are related—part of one creation.

When Jack showed Bennett how to cup his hands to receive the pine siskin, Bennett was intensely focused and a bit nervous. A pine siskin is a small bird—a kind of finch—mostly brown with yellow streaks. It weighs just fifteen grams—the same as three tea-spoons of salt. And though the bird, unlike salt, could not dissolve in water and change its form, she did seem to dissolve, or disap-pear into the air, when she felt an opening in the sweaty, uncertain cage Bennett had made with his hands. The siskin stayed still for two or three seconds but seemed to know Bennett was trying to free her before he did. As soon as she sensed the slightest opening, she burst through the limp, warm bars of his fingers—even before he could lift them—and vanished into the trees. Bennett looked stunned by what he and the bird had done. The siskin had opened Bennett's hand, and his eyes.

Later Jack caught a broad-tailed hummingbird, put it in a small silver sleeve to still its wings, turned it upside down, banded it, pulled it out of the sleeve, and put it in my daughter's open hand for release. This bird weighs three grams—less than a single penny. You could mail eight of them to a friend in an envelope with one U.S. postage stamp. Tessa was surprised by its delicacy, but more so by how it lay stock still in her open hand rather than flying away. I had never seen a hummingbird that was not humming, so its stillness also disturbed me. The bird presumed it was trapped. "It doesn't know that it's free," Jack said.

This line caught and held me. I loved the metaphor and the human implications, and so abruptly stopped worrying about the actual bird and focused on what I could do with the idea: we, too, ignore or misread the air and light and temperatures of our lives and thus never realize that we can fly away at any minute and become who we were meant to be. We are trapped by our own delusions, bound by our self-absorbed routines and the lures of affluence, of a consumer culture that—

And then Tessa dropped her hand a bit and the bird flew away, humming into the woods like a prehistoric insect awakened from the dead. As I watched it hover in the distance, it struck me that my personification of the bird's freedom, and of how it knows things, had a lure of its own.

Hummingbirds don't speak English. So I have no idea how or if it "knows" it is free, or even what that would mean. But an ornithologist later told me that banding a hummingbird is a severe physical stress that it can experience only as predation. And the restraint and turning of the birds during banding disturbs their semicircular ear canals and literally puts them out of balance. In other words, the bird could not recognize its "freedom," because it was temporarily disabled by its capture.

At this point it seems I should condemn bird banding as mistreatment of birds. It is, in a way. But it's also a useful means of studying bird populations and biology. And I could dismiss the magical encounter between the birds and the children as abusive. But I don't want to. One thing is clear though: the relatedness I spoke of is one sided—human centered. Wild birds don't feel connected to the person who traps and measures and bands them. And what I experienced as an inspiring moment of connection to the natural world, the birds likely perceived as a threat to their lives.

But in spite of this seeming naïveté, I don't think there's anything wrong with personifying nonhuman life, with trying to imagine what a hummingbird or coyote or colony of ants is thinking. Rather, it can be a good thing. Just as it may be useful to create metaphors to make the mystery of the Wild more knowable. Why not imagine the earth as our mother—as faithful and patient, but sick and exhausted? Because as unscientific or convenient or romantic as all this may seem, it's one of the few ways people have always tried to imagine, and thus to believe, that we are related, that we belong to Creation. And we have to start somewhere.

All of which brings me back here, to Bennett in the backyard. This is where we're starting: four house sparrows are scratching in the feed when a male cardinal drops out of nowhere like a shiny fire engine pulling up to a working-class bar. As the drab huddle of chattering sparrows makes way for the noble bird, I get a hunch about its name, which I've never thought of before.

Yeah, I was right; it's in the guide. Due to the male cardinal's stiff triangular crest and bright red feathers, the bird is named after its Catholic Church namesake. I tell Bennett this, and we begin to wonder whether the naming has anything to do with its behavior. Does the good father have an elevated sense of morality? When he flies away, I imagine he is off to address a flock of sinful starlings— to hold a chirpy mass in some huge lilac bush with a communion of mulberry juice and crickets. But instead he flies to his mate, who is perched and singing on a nearby elm branch. He feeds her the seed he has brought her.

This is impressive behavior, though I don't tell Bennett that human cardinals are single and celibate. Nor how amused I am by the clutch of house finches that have now gathered around the feeder. Whenever the cardinal returns to the feeder, they all quickly drop to the ground to gobble up the tiny grains he scatters on them in an odd sort of baptism. Or is it a rain of alms?

"Look, he's kicking the food to them," Bennett says.

"Yeah," I say. "And they seem thankful."

Later in the day, Bennett and I return to the patio. Two robins, a nuthatch, and a few sparrows are all having a quiet snack when a raucous gang of grackles arrive, crashing the bird feeders like drunk conventioneers who can't believe they've stumbled onto a free smorgasbord. It takes a minute for Bennett to figure out that the birds are grackles and not starlings. The guide helps: grackles walk on the ground—actually put one foot in front of the other—but starlings don't. Like robins and many other birds, they hop. We both like this—identifying the birds by behavior rather than color—seeing more than the most obvious markers.

"I count twenty-four, or maybe twenty-five," Bennett says. He watches the birds intently, but unlike me, he is not concerned about their aggression. We try to distinguish the males from the females and the juvenile birds from the mature birds. It's difficult, but the longer we watch, the more we see. Bennett reads from the guidebook that grackles sometimes eat sparrows and finches and their own young. This fun fact makes me long for the return of the cardinals—or perhaps a goldfinch or even the rare bluebird—something with a little more color and better manners. But they don't come back. The grackles empty both feeders in half an hour.

❧

The next day a storm window I was cleaning in front of the house comes apart in my hands, the sill completely rotten. So I buy some wood at the lumberyard and get out the miter saw to build a new one. While measuring the opening and scraping off the old paint, I get a feeling someone is watching me. Whenever I turn to look at the yew bush behind me, something rustles and flutters away just before I can see it. Then I get a glimpse—a flap of red: a male cardinal. Curious, I poke around in the bush and pull back a branch to find a nest with three babies—three scrawny bundles of bone and skin and down. The cardinal parents, just a few feet above me in a mulberry tree, begin to scold, so I back off.

The nest is right in front of a living room window, so I set up a folding chair inside as an observation post. We can plainly see the birds through the glass—like we have one of those hidden research cameras—but due to the nest's location, the birds can't see us.

We all love watching the cardinal family. Abby notes that they have three kids, just like our family. But theirs is more interesting—the way the father snatches worms and bugs from the grass and regurgitates them into the gaping beaks, and the way the mother protects the babies with her body, even in the pouring rain, shaking off the cold and wet. Yet there is one small, wonderful thing we have in common with the cardinal family: due to hormonal changes during nesting, the feathers of the mother's underside fall out and are replaced by a thin layer of down that recedes to reveal her hot, bare belly, which she spreads over the eggs during incubation, and over the nestlings during brooding. There are no feathers between a mother bird and her offspring; she is skin on skin with the newborns.

We check the cardinals every day.

"Look how little they are," Abby says. "How long before they can fly?"

"I'm not sure," I say. "Maybe a week?"

"I think it depends on how much they eat," Bennett says.

Abby looks it up in our ancient World Book encyclopedia: "Ten to twelve days, and then they can start another nest."

One morning, Tessa is sitting in the observation chair before school. "I just feel good whenever I see them," she says. I don't ask what she means, because I know. I think we all do. It feels good to remember, even for a few minutes, that we aren't all there is, that we are related to these small creatures, and all of us part of something bigger.

Soon we notice that one cardinal nestling is weak and not getting much food. He is dead in three days. The other two, stomping on their dead sibling as they feed, become so big in the next week that they barely fit in the nest. The day I install the new storm window, both are perched on the nest's rim with a kind of crazed adolescent determination in their eyes that would have scared the hell out of me if they were my kids. But neither of their parents is around. And I thought I had seen the mother a couple of houses down, already working on a new nest in a forsythia bush. How was the father supposed to feed these birds, and his partner, if she was starting a new nest down the block?

After I tap the window in, I walk over to get a better look at the wild-eyed birds-on-the-verge. I lift a branch to see them better and one abruptly jumps—fluttering, but mainly falling into a jungle of weeds and creepers five feet below. The absent father appears out of nowhere—loudly chirping and hopping madly around the spot in the thicket where his kid had gone down. I feel awful, as I had caused the crisis. My curiosity had prompted the bird's terror. Or had it? Perhaps the bird was just jumpy and any movement would have prompted him. A minute later, the other fledgling launches himself, also crashing somewhere in the weeds and creating an-other catastrophe for his dad.

Somehow, this all gets me thinking about Tessa learning to drive next year. And about myself, watching helplessly from the curb as she waves good-bye before accidentally flooring it and fish-tailing away. But by then it would be too late to help her, or to change her instinct to leave. Just as it would be two years later, when she departs for college. And though we might worry, we have an advantage over the cardinals—she will begin and finish on solid ground. And when she has mastered "flying" she will not disap-pear, but will still be a part of our family. Unlike the cardinals, our family can be a locus of home for Tessa for her whole life. At least I hope it will be.

Though I know that relationships between parents and their young can weaken and fail. So can a marriage. Half of them *do* fail. Some in our species mate for life, but many don't. People are also subject to instinct. Go to any bar on Friday night and watch our behavior—the colors, scents, dances, and noises we use to attract a mate. Some will choose to mate with many partners over a life, forming various kinds of families. A twice- or thrice-divorced or separated woman or man may have two or three broods to nurture, and may choose to seek yet another partner. Though I have not chosen that path, I appreciate the varied models of family—as well as the challenges of a lifelong partnership. A divorced friend of mine who calls marriage "unnatural" also sometimes reminds me of the bird species most associated with mating for life: the loons.

I look around in the bramble to see if I can find the lost fledglings, but then remember that I caused the problem, that they don't need any more of my help. So I go around back to fill the feeders with sunflower seeds. Maybe the cardinal, the good father, will recognize my offering as an act of contrition.

That night I read about cardinal behavior in a different bird guide, and again remembered that what I know determines what I can see. Cardinals always leave the nest before they can fly well, hopping around on the ground for another five or six days. The father continues to feed them until they are big enough to really take flight. The mother, however, usually leaves by this time to start a new brood.

The next day Carol and I see the male cardinal only once, and presume he's feeding the two fledglings in seclusion. The day after that, he disappears for good. So I go out to examine the nest. The dead sibling has been kicked out into the window well below. But oddly, there is a single unhatched egg in the nest none of us had seen—cream colored with small brown blotches. It is light, as if the yolk has dried up. I keep it.

ಞ

After watching these birds with Carol and the kids for ten days, I thought my cardinal encounters had ended for the year. But the very next weekend, I happened on another active nest near the farmhouse in Michigan. Though this one was different, what you might call an alternative family.

From a distance, I watch a large red male coming and going to a well-hidden nest in the middle of an arbor vitae bush, clearly feeding its nestlings. Hoping to get another hidden-camera angle on the birds, I climb about halfway up a huge silver maple tree whose limbs drape over the nest. There are three nestlings—about the same size and color as those we observed at home. The male cardinal is catching grasshoppers in the ditch along the road, chewing them up, and then regurgitating them into the gaping beaks. After three of these feeding runs, he disappears, and I wait for Mrs. Cardinal to appear. But she never does.

I call home and tell whomever will listen—Abby this time—that I've found a cardinal nest near the farmhouse and that I am going to set up another viewing station—this one in a tree. Abby is curious.

"What are you going to do if it rains?" she asks.

"I'll go inside and watch from the porch."

"Can you see the nest from that angle?"

"Yeah, I think so." But that's when I can hear that she has friends over—someone plunking on the piano and shrieking with laughter. So I get off the line.

"I'll keep you posted," I say.

"'Bye, Daddy."

Just after the call, a small bird with a dark, brownish head and back, white breast, and orangey shoulders flies over from across the road and lands on the nest. Is that a towhee? The color doesn't seem bright enough. Oh—it's a female, more subdued. But what the hell? I don't get it. Is this a mixed marriage? As I watch the towhee adjust herself on the nest, I get more excited and begin to wonder what those nestlings will become. What will they turn into? A brood of towdinals—feathered analogues of the labradoodle?

Wait a second. Wouldn't I know if such things were possible? Wouldn't I have seen red-breasted blue jays or red-headed starlings? Or was this the first time it had ever happened? Maybe this was bigger than the sighting of the ivory-billed woodpecker!

I e-mail the ornithologist at the nearby University of Chicago and he says to get my camera, as I may have stumbled on a rare case of interspecific hybridity. I don't have a camera with me. But I keep watching. I spend the afternoon in my perch high above the nest with my notepad, and my binocs trained on the birds in question.

The female towhee remains on the nest, and the male cardinal appears every half hour or so to feed the little ones. The two birds seem to get along, but I somehow can't quite believe that the cardinal is the father. It just didn't make sense. And that's when it hits me. *Maybe he's gay.* Tired and bored from staring at the nest, I dream up the backstory.

Let's call him Roger. And her Kate. Roger and Kate were intimate but platonic friends in college—close in every way but one. Early on, before Kate knew, every time they touched—wings, beaks, a brushing of tail feathers—there was a tension. But it was different for each of them. For Kate, it was emotionally charged and full of what-ifs. For Roger, it was somehow comforting, reassuring. When Roger finally told Kate, she was both relieved and disappointed. But that intimate moment of revelation intensified and secured a friendship that lasted long past college. And so, after Kate found a mate and began her first brood, she instinctively called Roger, knowing he would love a shot at surrogate fatherhood. And she knew he would be easier to confide in, and more nurturing than Mark, the actual father, who though stunning in his plumage and flight speed, struggled to share his feelings, to be honest with her.

While I am dreaming all this up, Mark actually appears on the scene. Teetering on a small branch about twenty feet below my perch, and just five feet above Kate and the nest, he's in perpetual alarm mode, chirping like a maniac. But Kate doesn't seem to notice. A little while later, she leaves the nest and joins him on his perch. Seemingly relieved, Mark finally stops his frenetic chirping.

Then Roger appears again. His crimson feathers are immaculate, his crest impeccably combed. After pushing more mashed bugs into the wide-open beaks, he leaves. Then Kate returns to the nest and Mark starts the crazed chirping again. This goes on through four more cycles over the next two hours. But Mark, the real father, never feeds the nestlings nor sits on the nest, and is constantly twitching and bothered. What's happening here?

After Mark's appearance, and after convincing myself that Roger is gay, I begin to doubt the possibility of a towdinal. Mark is clearly the father. So the next morning I drive to the Bridgman public library and e-mail my new observations to the ornithologist. He has a different answer this time: not interspecific hybridity, but interspecific feeding. He sends a link to an article from the *Journal of Field Ornithology*.[2]

The article, the only inclusive study on the topic, reviews 140 cases of this behavior going back to 1900. The author, Marilyn Muszalski Shy, identifies several reasons birds might nurture and feed birds from a different species. There is no mention of gay cardinals (or lesbian blue jays), but two of the rationales seem possible: one, the nest of the "helper bird," or its brood, was destroyed, or, two, the helper bird is mateless. Roger's original nest and brood may have been blown out in a bad storm. (There were winds of sixty to seventy miles per hour here last week.) Or perhaps he was unable to attract a mate, or she was killed during the incubation period. In either case, instinctively driven to feed and nurture, Roger likely sought out an active nest in his neighborhood—the Mark and Kate Towhee family.

Were Roger a person, we might say he was compassionate, or that he was working out his grief in a positive way. But he's a bird, so we say he's following instinct. I don't quite buy this, because love is partly instinct. And research going back to Charles Darwin—the first scientist to seriously study animal emotion—has argued that other animals do have emotions, that a cat approaching a robin would prompt that robin's fear, and his *e-motion*—movement. "The lower animals, like man," Darwin wrote, "manifestly feel pleasure and pain, happiness and misery."[3]

But primary inborn emotions, such as the robin's fight-or-flight response, are different from secondary emotions, which are not auto-responses in the brain, but processed and nuanced—the individual must consider what to do about them. The point is no one knows for sure if birds grieve, or if they experience the emotional gymnastics of love. Even so, I'm going out on a silver maple limb—with Mark and Roger and Kate—and will just say it: I believe. I think birds love.

My evidence: very little—a few years of occasional birdwatching, some articles and books, and some stories from birders about crow funerals and monogamous loons and cheating warblers. But after trying harder to see nature in new ways with Thoreau, and with my kids, my thinking has started to shift. I'm slowly losing faith in the old models—in seeing is believing—and beginning to wonder whether believing is seeing.

In Shy's article, many examples might prompt readers to personify birds—to think that birds love. In 1913, a nestful of baby kingbirds was observed calling loudly after a bad electrical storm. The kingbird parents had disappeared. A wood pewee found and fed the orphans for ten days until they fledged. In 1924, a mateless house wren fed three black-headed grosbeaks until they fledged and then fed a nestful of house sparrows. And there are several other cases of orphaned nestlings being cared for by whomever lives in the neighborhood. Such examples make Shy wonder about the evolutionary advantages of such behavior. She doesn't find many. "Being raised by foster parents can lead to later problems," she writes. "When a pair of common terns raised a herring gull, it did not behave like a normal gull."

The human being is the only species that has ever tried to be "normal," or to determine what that means. But *normal* is just as elusive and hard to define as *love*. Which is perhaps why there is no such thing as *normal love*—with birds or people. And thank goodness. What bird or person would want to be in a love that had been normed—studied and made predictable and reliable?

All of which brings me back to my thesis: *birds love*. Here's how I know (and I'm calling this field research): Yesterday I was in my perch in the silver maple, with the sun streaming through the leaves in long, flickering shafts of light. When I put out my hand to touch one, Mark's head swiveled to look at me. But he stayed quiet, because Kate was perched right next to him. They were watching Roger feed grasshoppers to the nestlings—who now looked big enough to fledge. After he had fed the birds, instead of disappearing across the road into the woods as usual, Roger flew up to the same branch as Mark and Kate and perched there, just a few feet away. They all seemed at home somehow, like they had temporarily worked things out. There was a new calm.

Until a few seconds later, when they all went nuts—on alarm mode—with more chirping and cheeping that I thought three birds could make. On the ground far below me, and just a few feet below the birds, a large yellow tomcat slunk under the bush. He was in the nest almost as soon as I realized what was about to happen. Roger dove at the cat in a dangerous swoop—within a few inches of the cat's claws. But the cat was too excited by the nestlings to notice. Then Kate and Mark tried their own gallant dives. But they were also ignored. The cat stuffed one of the nestlings in his mouth and chomped it up while pinning the other two under his claws. Kate and Mark dive-bombed again. This time Kate grazed the cat's ear with one of her feet. But still no response. A red trickle as bright as Roger's feathers dripped from the corner of the cat's mouth. And then he was gone—quickly crossing the road with the two twitching birds crammed in his open mouth—vanishing into the ditch weeds. A minute or so later, Roger and Kate and Mark finally stopped their crazed hopping and cheeping.

I can't know what those three birds felt while watching their offspring being slaughtered and eaten from a few feet away. But I know what I saw from my perch above them: a frantic helplessness in their fluttering bodies and bobbing heads and crazed chirping. In the shiny beads of their eyes, I read one thing: desperation. Maybe the desperation was partly mine, and maybe I'm relying too much on my imagination rather than on facts and research. But I'm coming to think that there are as many ways to see, and to grieve, and to love, as there are people, and birds. My only option that day was just to be there—to watch and belong to that moment of holy terror.

⅔

None of the birds returned the next day. So I went to inspect the nest, and was startled to again find one unbroken egg nestled against the damp sticks—cream colored with small, brown blotches, just like the cardinal egg. So now what? Was I to believe that the slaughtered nestlings were cardinals, and that Roger was the unfortunate father? If so, what happened to his mate, and why had Kate and Mark stepped in? Or was this a mixed clutch, meaning both cardinal and towhee eggs had been laid in the same nest?

I e-mail the ornithologist. He says cardinal and towhee eggs look a lot alike, but cardinal eggs are slightly larger. His eyes might have seen the difference in color and pattern between the two eggs, but I didn't have a clue. After a few minutes though, I could recognize the size difference. The Glen Ellyn cardinal egg was slightly larger than the Michigan towhee egg. So I presume that my original story might hold up—that Roger might have lost his mate, or his nest, or both. And, motivated by a lot of instinct, a bit of emotion, and a speck of reason, he had been wandering through the woods looking for other birds to care for, other birds to love.

SUMMER

This is June, the month of grass and leaves. . . .
I feel a little fluttered in my thoughts, as if I might
be too late. Each season is but an infinitesimal point.
It no sooner comes than it is gone. It has no duration.
It simply gives a tone and hue to my thought.

HENRY DAVID THOREAU, *Journal*[1]

Chapter 6

Cabin Fever
Alone and Lonely

Why should I feel lonely? Is not our planet in the Milky Way?

HENRY DAVID THOREAU, *Walden*[1]

Tonight, after a good day of writing in the cabin, I decide to walk into town to have dinner. There aren't many businesses in Sawyer: Cooney's Hardware, Schlipps drugstore, the post office, a small grocery, a laundry–coffee shop–Internet café, and Rosie's Grill, a beat-up bar that offers dollar hamburgers and dollar drafts on Tuesday nights.

After I order my burger and Bud, a middle-aged guy in denim overalls sits down next to me and makes small talk. An unemployed carpenter, he has just found a month's work as a framer building a casino in New Buffalo, a popular tourist town eight miles south of here on the lake.

"What do *you* do?" he finally asks.

I usually say, "I'm an English teacher," but since I'd actually been writing all day, I don't. "At the moment, I'm a writer," I say. He seems amused, and takes a long, thoughtful sip of his beer.

And then, instead of looking at me directly, as he has been doing, he looks straight ahead, speaking to my reflection in the bar mirror in front of us. "I wouldn't never want to do that," he says.

"Why?" I ask, now also talking to the mirror, to the unshaven face reflected behind the row of liquor bottles.

"Because you guys are never happy," he says.

Though I ask twice, he won't say why he thinks that. But it rings true. I have come to Rosie's Grill, after all, because I'm lonely. I'd been pecking at my laptop all day in the cabin like a nervous grackle trying to find a few grains of seed in the grass. For me, even at its best, writing is an intensely lonely work of love; it can inspire and depress at the same time. Last week, while reading Thoreau's *Journal,* I thought I had found a moment where he seemed sympathetic with this idea. He mentions a "certain fertile sadness." *Fertile* didn't surprise me; *sadness* did—an unusual word for Mr. Positive. But then I kept reading. It is a sadness, he wrote, that he "would not avoid, but rather earnestly seek. It is positively joyful. . . . It saves my life from being trivial."[2]

When this joyful sadness wells up in Thoreau's work, I feel an odd mix of envy and admiration about the exuberance he always finds—both in the woods and in the words. In *Walden,* he discovers joy in everything from a stinking, decaying horse carcass to a weedy bean field.

Though I don't readily find joy in sadness, I'm trying to read that way, to think more like Thoreau, to see light merging with darkness, hope lingering in shadow. But it's not working. I keep getting stuck in the mud of my trivial life: Should Bennett try out for travel soccer, or is he too young? Why is our sewer line clogged again when I just rodded it? How did our entire yard become a creeping Charlie plantation? When are Carol and I ever going to have a night to ourselves?

After a second beer, I walk down Flynn Road in the darkness back to the cabin. The full moon and the stars—spilt like sugar across the black abyss of the heavens—keep reminding me of what

I am—a creature, one of billions, slowly making his way across the surface of this big, blue spinning marble. Yet it is less a sense of isolation than of belonging. With the cornfields and vineyards glowing in the moonlight all around me, and the wind playing familiar hymns on the oak and elm, I feel more at home and less alone at that moment than I have for a long time.

That is until I trip over a roadkill raccoon and tumble onto the asphalt. When I look closer, I am startled to see he is still alive, still twitching, the blood warm, his eyes open. What am I supposed to do? I want to get him off the road so he won't get hit again, but what if he's playing possum and saving up his energy for one last vengeful lunge at the human species?

I touch the top of his head with my shoe. No. He's almost gone. As I grab his thick tail, lift all fifteen or so pounds of him off the road, and gently lay him in the ditch, I can hear him breathing. This both startles and troubles me. The labored suck and hiss of his breath sounds so much like Bennett in the night with a head cold that I soon find myself kneeling down in the damp weeds in a sort of wordless prayer—for forgiveness, I think. Then I leave him there to die and walk back to the cabin.

At dawn the next morning I wade back into my work, trying to read these woods and *Walden* as one braided experience. Today it's Thoreau's "Solitude" chapter—a brief ten pages, but troubling. It's so full of the elation his aloneness brings him that I don't quite believe it, or want to. And in this passage sadness is not joyful, but vulgar, a sign of weakness:

> Nothing can rightly compel a simple and brave man to a vulgar sadness. While I enjoy the friendship of the seasons I trust that nothing can make life a burden to me.[3]

Being neither simple, nor brave, this kind of sadness I understand. Even now, as I read, I find myself again walking out onto the rickety bridge I have strung between *alone* and *lonely*—stumbling into one of those precarious unfocused moments where I so fear slipping on a loose board that I can't see the forest *or* the trees. I look straight ahead, stare blankly at Thoreau's words and then at the woods, unable to read either.

I try to call Carol on my cell. It's an old phone I got free, a thick, heavy one. It works about a third of the time in the cabin. Today it shows four bars of reception. That's good. It's ringing. Abby's taped voice comes on, but it's garbled and chopped up. Then the same voice interrupts itself in real time, this one warm and alive: "Daddy? Is that—?" Then silence. Then three bars of reception. Then none. Then a red, blinking stop sign and the words "No Signal." I walk out of the cabin and the woods into the clearing near the farmhouse and try again. Still out of range. Why did I even try? Now they'll wonder why I called, what's wrong.

Cabin fever: the anxiety caused by physical isolation in a remote natural setting; the intense desire to return to the comforts of technology and human interaction. How ironic that I have contracted it in the cozy little abode we built as a retreat from the chaos of normal life. And how odd that the term "cabin fever" may have originated during the era of my guru of solitude—Thoreau.

In the nineteenth century, Midwestern homesteaders lived literally off the beaten path, and much farther from an actual road. These families were so isolated from commerce and community that they could be snowed in their cabins for months at a time, their sanity tested as they waited for the spring thaw. Willa Cather, O. E. Rolvaag, Rose Wilder Lane, and other writers powerfully chronicled this experience—the physical and emotional isolation of the early settlers on the Great Plains. The land was so immense, the quiet so deep, that they sometimes drowned in it—in a wild, unending loneliness.

But this kind of cabin fever—physical isolation in the natural world caused by weather and roadlessness—has now all but disappeared in the United States.[4] And ironically, the one small thing I and other overwhelmed "moderns" have in common with Thoreau is that we go to the woods *seeking* isolation in nature. We are not snowed in. Our solitude is chosen, carefully planned. We flee the material comfort and frantic convenience of our high-tech lives. We don't trust that the digitized GPS voice in our cars will tell us where we need to go. We are looking for something else. Something we cannot purchase at the mall or order on the Internet. But what is it?

I try to call home again. This time Carol picks up. I get only about every other syllable but still understand her: "Everyth . . . is O. . . . Kid . . . are fine. How . . . writ . . . go . . . ? What time will . . . ome . . . tom . . . row?" I tell her I'm fine and will be home in time to pick the kids up at school the next day. From her tone, she seems in good spirits. Even the brief, broken exchange of info is a relief to me.

I step outside. I'm not sure why, but now the dark clouds gathering above me feel less like a closing in than an opening up, as if it is a darkness that could also somehow illuminate. What or how, I don't know.

But I know that darkness is as varied as light, that they are not opposites but the same thing in varied degrees: the growing presence of one is simply the growing absence of the other. I first learned this in a botanical-art class while doing a pencil drawing of a sycamore seed pod. Our teacher told us that the variation of light and dark in the pod is just as complex in the shadow it casts, and just as beautiful. She told us to always look at the darkness as carefully as the light—the delicate graduation of the penumbra (partial shadow) to the umbra (full shadow) to the pod itself.

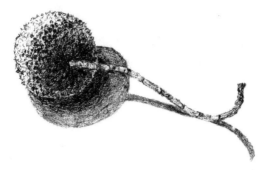

This image reminds me of a cottonwood tree next to the cabin. It's an odd tree. Over the last decade it has erupted through a small opening amid the dense stand of white pine. The top quarter of the tree now rises ten feet above the pine canopy and has a monopoly on the sunlight. So the top half of the tree thrives. But the bottom half, which is in the thick, cool darkness, has some dead limbs and few leaves. So imagine my surprise yesterday when, after a storm, I walked out to find a blotchy white shadow at the base of the cottonwood. Parts of it had fallen in soft clumps in the crooks of the pine whorls, but more than enough had been cast through the maze of branches to form the silky pool around the trunk— about ten feet in diameter. If the tree had more space and light, the wind would have done its work and broken up the seed bundles and dispersed them widely over our land. But instead, this albino shadow—so stark amid the darkness of the woods that I use it to find my way to the cabin that night.

The familiar rhythm in the grass and the cold drops on my arm end my daydreaming. The wind picks up and blows the rain into sheets that pelt the roof in waves. Wet and shivering, I go back inside, dry off, and return to *Walden*.

The more I read, the clearer it becomes that the goal of Thoreau's retreat was less disconnection with human community than reconnection with a wider community—to be "part and parcel of Nature,"[5] an inhabitant. He doesn't equate his aloneness, his *solitude* (a spiritual state), with physical separation from people. "Solitude is not measured by the miles of space that intervene between a man and his fellows," he writes. His cabin was just a twenty-minute walk from Concord, which he visited "every day or two . . . to hear some of the gossip."[6]

If the cabin was an escape, it was an escape to *less*—to less noise and distraction, to fewer choices and obligations. It was also an escape to *more*—to more presence and balance, to a more deliberate life.

I find the reference, the well-known sentence that defines Thoreau's purpose: "I went to the woods because I wished to live deliberately, to front only the essential facts of life, and see if I could not learn what it had to teach, and not, when I came to die, discover that I had not lived."[7]

Thoreau's deliberate life, his attentiveness and presence, gave him a sense of his own scale, of his small but essential place in the balance of Nature. This is the cabin fever that burns in him—not an anxious *longing* for escape, but a wondrous sense of *belonging* to Creation.

Even so, now, as I peruse *Walden,* I'm fixed on what Thoreau doesn't say, on the fever that is missing, on the inevitable spirals of loneliness. But they aren't there—with one exception, the one weak moment he committed to ink:

> I have never felt lonesome . . . but once . . . when, for an hour, I doubted if the near neighborhood of man was not essential to a serene and healthy life. To be alone was something unpleasant.[8]

Only one hour of loneliness in his two years at the cabin? Unlikely. And his journal and letters suggest otherwise. But maybe it doesn't matter, because *Walden* is less reportage than art, less fact than truth. And it is his recovery from this supposedly rare instance of loneliness that most inspires readers—including me.

That day, amid a gentle rain, Thoreau suddenly recognizes what he calls the "sweet and beneficent society in Nature. . . . Every little pine needle expanded and swelled with sympathy and befriended me. I was so distinctly made aware of the presence of something kindred to me . . . that I thought no place could ever be strange to me again."[9]

Thoreau's awareness of this sacred Belonging, of this Wildness, deeply attracts me. In part because I want to believe it can be found anywhere it is sought: in this cabin, amid this replanted pine forest and soybean field turned meadow, and all along our chemical- and sediment-choked river. And even in the old creek bed, where discarded tractor parts and kitchen appliances someone dumped sixty years ago are rusting into dirt, turning back into the earth.

But I also want to believe it is part of the rest of my life—most of my life—including my marriage and family. And as the darkness gathers around me tonight in the woods, and a few stars try to penetrate a thin wall of cloud, I can't help but wonder whether this is at the root of the unspoken loneliness I sometimes sense in Thoreau. I may have read too much *Walden* today, or I may be projecting, or fishing for points of connection where they don't exist, but I wonder how marriage and children would have affected Thoreau's otherwise deliberate life—if they would have restrained or liberated him as a person and as a writer. How would Thoreau have written *Walden* with a wife and three kids?

I got married and had children "because I wished to live deliberately, to front only the essential facts of life, and see if I could not learn what it had to teach, and not, when I came to die, discover that I had not lived." Thoreau might not be amused by this playful jab. But it suggests why his cabin fever can be both inspiring and confusing for readers like me. I'm left wondering how he would have negotiated a much different kind of wildness—how he would have balanced the deep compromises marriage and parenting require. How would his fierce commitment to leisure and his stubborn idealism have endured his children's late-night sickness, or his partner's request for him to get a job and earn a bit of money? How would the immense patience he shows in the woods—his intense listening to all the voices there—have translated to the family dinner table?

Perhaps those are not fair questions. Some Thoreau scholars would say, "You have to accept Thoreau on his own terms." Or, "Thank God he *didn't* marry and have children, or we wouldn't have *Walden* and the *Journal.*" But most readers, like me, are not scholars. We view great books partly through the lens of our own lives. So although marriage and children were not part of the life Thoreau chose, their absence in his life is also a kind of presence. Readers are curious about where his passions actually lay, and about how and who he loved. Did his fervent love of nature and his vibrant friendships with a handful of men supplant his desires for a life partner or to have children? Or did he sometimes long to find the intense physical love he had for the woods, for the swamp and the pond, in a *human* relationship—to find not just an intellectual or familial love, but *eros*, a deeply romantic and sexual love? Maybe this was also a part of the seeking, of the Wild fever that drove him—an awkward, rarely expressed part that was diminished but never quite relieved by the swell of a pine needle, or a cool blanket of rain.

Chapter 7

In the Time of the Cicada
Patience and Passion

Our most glorious experiences are a kind of regret. Our regret
is so sublime we may mistake it for triumph. It is the painful
plaintive sad surprise of our Genius remembering our past lives
and contemplating what is possible.

HENRY DAVID THOREAU, *Journal*[1]

As the school year winds down, we're already getting a taste of
summer. It hit 80 degrees this afternoon. So late tonight, after the
kids are in bed, Carol and I sit out on the patio to enjoy the warm
air and some red wine. But it's not as relaxing as we'd like. There is
a problem, something we need to talk about.

We lean back into our plastic lawn chairs to gather our thoughts
when we both hear it—a faint clicking. Then the hosta leaves start
to move. We look down at the hostas and then back up at each
other. We know what it is. We kneel over the sound until we see
one. They are rising again. After seventeen years of waiting in the
darkness and sipping on tree roots, the cicadas are emerging, and
we are both on all fours in the dirt watching them.

Last week I noticed their exit holes in our flowerbeds—the

openings to their finger-size mud chimneys. Soon, the cicada nymphs became living heat sensors, slipping up and down the snug chambers like little pistons, first sampling the air and then retracting into their earthy sleeves. They tested and retested the temperature like this, over and over, waiting for the moment when their body would "know" that the soil had reached 65 degrees, chemically signaling it was time to leave.

We return to our chairs and the conversation we haven't had. Carol needs surgery. She has fibroid tumors that cause enough bleeding during her monthly cycle to be dangerous. She gets dizzy just going up the stairs. While visiting a friend with the kids last week, she passed out in a pool of blood and they rushed her to the hospital for a transfusion. It could have easily happened while she was zooming down the highway. And it's not the first time she has passed out.

She needs to have her uterus removed. That's where the tumors are. We don't want more kids, and she can keep her ovaries, so she won't be catapulted into menopause, but understandably, her worry and sense of loss is deep. She fears that the surgery will not only end her ability to create life but also somehow undo her as a woman.

I try to reassure her with the research pamphlets: "The surgery rarely has significant impact on sexual activity or experience."

"'Rarely' and 'significant' are just not good enough," Carol says. I know she's right, which is why I remind her of what the OB/GYN had said: There's little choice. It had been life threatening. She needs to get it done before her next cycle—within three weeks.

I pour more wine. We both take sips and listen for the emerging cicada. Thousands more are stirring in the earth below us, all getting ready to crawl out of their skins, to molt from nymphs into adults. Their soft, white bodies will harden and darken as they open their wings and creep up the forsythia and the maple and elm trees that line our yard. In their wake, they leave crisp, brown shells clinging to the bark and leaves like a sepia snapshot of their own transformation.

The next morning we talk more about the surgery. "Maybe I could be really careful, triple the iron supplements, tank up on liver and onions, and put it off for a while," Carol says. "We have done it before you know."

"Yeah," I say, "but it's always harrowing. Each month has been worse than the last. Your body just doesn't absorb enough iron to make up for the loss."

When I say *loss,* the corners of her mouth tighten and she sighs. "I know. But I just really don't want to do it."

At this point, she needs me to say, "Don't worry—it's going to be all right." But in twenty years of marriage, I've never quite learned how to say that at the right times. So instead of consoling, I continue to build my case, stupidly reminding her about the last episode, about how they all could have been killed if she had been driving. This doesn't help. Nor does the fact that I think she *knows:* my failure to console is not just my typical oversight or self-absorption. I'm not sure about this either. I'm worried too.

Over the next few days, the cicada population explodes: up to a million per acre—maybe 300,000 in our backyard. Some of our neighbors are repulsed by the swarms of bugs clinging to their bushes and flowers, or falling out of trees into their hair during an evening stroll. But others, like me, find them miraculous: seventeen years of patience, of darkness, followed by a few weeks of passion, of sunlight and sex. Each night, I sit outside and listen to the newest arrivals move through the grass and leaves: chaotic platoons of red-eyed soldiers crunching over thousands of their own brittle casings. Then up the trees they march to wait for the sun and sing for a mate.

On a bright, clear day, the waves of sound from the male cicada are deafening, like huge fleets of low-flying bomber planes that just kept coming and coming. The drone can reach 95 decibels, at which point audiologists suggest going indoors to avoid hearing damage. Once, while I was mowing the lawn, hundreds of them started dive-bombing me, landing on my clothing and the mower. I didn't figure it out until a few days later that they were females attracted to the blare of the mower. To them, the whirring mower was saying the same things the male cicadas were: "Have sex with me!" "No, have sex with *me!*" "No me!" "No me!" "No me!"

The other animals in our yard care less about mating than eating. The bird feeder has been untouched ever since the cicadas arrived, as the cardinals and sparrows and blue jays gorge themselves on the plump delicacies. The backyard becomes a groaning smorgasbord for everything from dogs to raccoons to chipmunks. Even people see the cicada as an opportune, short-lived cuisine. The recipes are all clear-cut: you collect the cicada right after they molt and before they harden, and then boil or fry them. Basically, follow whatever recipe you're using, and then stir in the cooked cicada "to taste." They have a nutty flavor. I tried some cicada-oatmeal cookies at a picnic, where I heard about a few other recipes I "just had to try": curried cicada and chickpeas, cicada-portobello quiche, and German chocolate–cicada cake.

On the day of the surgery, Carol's mom arrives at 6:00 a.m. to watch the kids. We throw our bag in the car and leave for the hospital. We are both pretty quiet on the thirty-minute drive. But Carol seems less tense, like she has shifted from worried resignation to guarded relief.

An hour after arriving at the hospital, Carol is gowned and wheeled away by a nurse to have her vitals taken. "Wait here," the nurse tells me. While I'm standing there, my mind wanders to the last time we were in a hospital together, seven years ago, for our son's birth. He was born fifteen minutes after we got there. I can still see the wild beauty of his emergence: the little blue head, the folded arms, the quick slip of the hips and legs—the abrupt journey from the wet, warm darkness into the dry, cold light of the world. And I remember Carol's fierce grunting and crying, and then laughing, as her deepest suffering and purest joy melded into one thing—life.

My daydream ends when the nurse returns with Carol lying on a gurney. It's time.

Carol says it first. "I love you." Then me. Her eyes are wet and tired.

"It's going to be OK," I say, trying to radiate confidence. And then, "This will be over before you know it."

"OK," Carol says, trying to smile. A kiss.

"See you soon," I say.

The surgery is supposed to take two hours. I watch TV in the waiting room. HBO is playing *Something's Gotta Give*. Jack Nicholson, a sixtysomething playboy dating a thirtysomething bombshell, falls in love with her mother (Diane Keaton) and in so doing recognizes that his physical longing for young women, for sexual affirmation that he is still virile and desirable, has prevented him from finding a deeper love.

The movie ends. I look at my watch. Three hours. Still no word. I ask the nurse to check to be sure everything is OK. She calls and five minutes later tells me everything is fine, just going slower than they had planned. Don't worry. These things are hard to predict.

I'm not sure I believe her. I keep watching TV and try not to think about it. The local news runs at the top of the hour. The lead-in story, not surprisingly, is "The Passion of the Cicada." It focuses on the physical transformation, the mating songs and egg laying, on that tiny fraction of the cicada's life we can hear and see. Though I find myself wondering about the part we can't see—the *patience* of the cicada, the ninety-nine percent of its life spent waiting in the darkness.

According to the story, the seeming imbalance between patience and passion in the cicada's life is useful. The rare cyclical emergence of the cicada evolved to overwhelm their predators (who simply can't eat them all) and to confound the shorter life cycles of other potential predators. The patience and passion has a purpose, and it has worked for a very long time: fossil records suggest cicada species have been around for a hundred million years.

But what concerns me this afternoon is a much younger species—*Homo sapiens*—and how we are to manage our own imbalance of passion and patience. And I'm wondering about the strange dissonance and resonance between these ideas. *Patience* and *passion*, words that seem to be near opposites, share a common Latin root, *pati*, meaning "to suffer" or "to endure." So what does suffering or enduring have to do with love and sex? Isn't love mainly about patience, and sex mainly about passion? Does the suffering come because the two are not interwoven in the relationship? Or because they are woven too tightly?

In mainstream culture *passion* is defined narrowly: "Follow your passion" to Aruba or to the Mercedes dealership. We have a passion for shopping, for desserts, for cheese, for Jesus, for horses, for paperweights, for pinball, for jazz, for nature. Enroll in Passion University at Passion.edu: "Holistic education for passionate living." Find fulfillment at Passion.com: "Sexy personals for passionate singles." Try the Passion Pill (an herbal alternative to Viagra) and "Put Passion back in your life!"

Here, passion seems to connote *im*patience—the drive to quench one's most pressing urges. It is part of love, but maybe not the part that sustains a relationship. Which is perhaps why there is little similarity between the love life of a cicada and that of a human being, between the blind magnetism of wild, last-minute bug sex and the sophisticated physical and emotional fine tunings of human lovemaking. A human, after all, could not wait in a dark, cold underworld for seventeen years before coming out in the final week of life for a few days of nonstop sex and egg laying. People move through the darkness and light, the shadows and shimmers of love, through moments of passion and patience, every day. And in so doing, they feel both suffering and its intimate partner, *joy.*

Four hours. Too long. When I get up to inquire again, the surgeon pushes through the swinging door in her powder-blue scrubs. A vibrant, attractive woman, she looks uncharacteristically tired and disappointed. Her hands are clean and dry, but there is a tiny splatter of blood on her cheek, and more on her shirt and shoes.

"We couldn't do it laparoscopically," she says. "Carol was bleeding too much. We had to open her up. It still went fine, but the healing will be much slower—weeks instead of days. The thing to remember is, no lifting or sexual activity for six weeks." They had hoped to section and remove the uterus through two small incisions, but it didn't go as planned. From the splatters and the tired look, I wonder how difficult it had actually been. I knew I'd never know. The doctor would never say. Still, I liked her—not too clinical or too chummy, yet compassionate. She tells me it will be two hours before Carol's out of recovery.

I go outside for a walk. The hospital is on Lake Michigan. In a garden along the lake, I stop at a bench under a magnolia tree that is somehow still blooming. The pink flowers are huge and dripping with dew. The stamens quiver in the wind, trying but failing to hold themselves erect against the strong gusts off the lake. Dozens of cicadas have molted and are climbing up the magnolia trunk. But for some reason many on this tree didn't make it. About half are dead, perhaps due to fertilizer and herbicides. Some have deformed wings or legs. And a few seem to have died at the moment of transformation—frozen as little bug statues with three-quarters of the body out of the husk.

I look more closely at one of these failed attempts. The prehistoric head and torso and forelegs of the emerging adult are poised in the air as if it is praying. A tiny piece of its exoskeleton is just barely hooked on the edge of its brown husk. But it is enough to hold the cicada in the shell of its past life, with its eyes fixed on the tree's crown, the destination it would not reach after seventeen years of preparation.

Should we lament that this cicada, now frozen in its death pose, knew neither sex nor love? Or that it didn't know the difference between the two? Or that in its last moment of life, its little tick of a brain couldn't and wouldn't remember all those years in the darkness, or try to measure their value against the present, or ponder on what its life had meant? Or perhaps we should instead admire the cicada's sense of time, the way it lives always and only in the present, without regret or second thoughts.

When they bring Carol into her room from recovery, she is still groggy from the anesthesia and pain meds. I reach over the bed rail and take her hand. She tries to smile. When she asks me how it went, I have to tell her about the change of plan: that they had to open her up, that the healing will take much longer. Some tears of sadness, then I'm not sure—perhaps resignation, maybe just exhaustion. Soon she falls back to sleep.

After four days, and another blood transfusion, they finally tell us we can leave. The morning we are to go home, as I'm packing the bag, the doctor and the nurse stop in separately to remind me what I've now been told eight or nine times: no lifting or sexual activity for six weeks. This strikes me as odd. I start to wonder whether they are going to ask me to sign something legally binding. As we are driving home down the interstate, I tell Carol I won't be surprised if we get a Big Brother–like taped recording at our house every four hours to remind me. I feign a digitized voice: "This is the hospital calling. Your wife has just had her uterus removed. Do not let her do any lifting. And DO NOT under any circumstances have sex with her." Carol, forgetting her incisions, guffaws at this. Her expression quickly turns to pain.

At home Carol cannot walk up the stairs, so we set her up in the family room, where she happily camps with coffee and books. The kids and I bring her food and enjoy taking care of her. The next morning I walk Bennett to school. On the way, we stop to marvel at a foot-high mound of brown cicada shells under a neighbor's tree. And below us, on the sidewalk, they are mating all over the place.

Bennett notices before me: "What are they doing, Daddy?"

"Mating," I say. "They're making more cicadas. The daddy is fertilizing the mommy's eggs, which are still inside her body."

That is all he wants to know. He doesn't ask me what *fertilize* means or how the male gets inside the female. Rather, he just picks a pair up to look at in his hand. It's amusing: the male doesn't mount the female, but sort of backs into her. They mate with their heads facing away from each other—tail to tail—kind of like a pushmi-pullyu in the Dr. Dolittle books.

After watching for a few seconds, Bennett has another question: "Who's winning? The mommy or the daddy?"

I have no idea. Bennett puts the tightly linked cicadas back down on the sidewalk, and they stumble into the grass. At that moment a starling swoops down in front of us and snatches them, gobbling down both the cicada who was looking down his throat and the one who was looking at the ground and never saw what hit him.

As we approach the school, I can't help but remember a summer day several years ago when Tessa and Abby discovered two raccoons mating on our back deck. The girls were both mesmerized and had their noses pressed against the window. I was standing behind them, and they didn't see me.

"What are they doing?" Abby asked her older sister. "What are they wrestling about?"

"They're making a baby," Tessa explained. "I saw some lions do it on TV. That's the daddy on top."

Midmorning, I bring Carol fresh coffee and open the window so she can hear the fevered wane of the cicada in the sunlight.

"Listen," I tease. "The cicada boys are taunting you."

"Tell them they'll have to wait six weeks," Carol says, "then I'll give them more than they can handle." We laugh. We are alone. The kids are all at school, and I don't have to be at work for an hour. I squeeze in close beside her on the sofa.

"This is nice," I say, "to actually be alone during the day."

"Yeah, it's nice," she says. But she is teary, and I'm not sure why.

That's when she reaches over and puts both of her hands on my face and pulls it close to hers, so we are almost nose to nose. And there, in a moment of passion, and patience, we try to answer with our eyes all the questions we didn't know how to ask, and hush the worries creeping up from the deep. It is as if we have again crawled out of some dark womb and into the sunlight, where everything is new and trying to be born.

Chapter 8

Mushrooms
Love and Sex

Like cuttlefish, we conceal ourselves, we darken the atmosphere
in which we move; we are not transparent. I pine for one to whom
I can speak *my first thoughts*. Thoughts which represent me truly,
which are no better or worse than I.

HENRY DAVID THOREAU, *Journal*[1]

By midsummer Carol has completely healed, and we are both
thankful. This morning she's swimming laps at the YMCA. I'm
sitting on the back porch drinking coffee, waiting for the kids to
wake up, and watching a pair of manic squirrels in an elm tree.
They are in a frenetic wrestling match, which is full of take-downs
and reversals. But no one ever gets pinned. He's on top. She pops
out. She's on top. He pops out and leaps to another tree. She follows. And it all continues as before. Squirrel foreplay looks ex-
hausting. The chipmunks are going at it too—in the grass and then
in our aluminum downspout. They thump around in the tinny
darkness for a while, tumble out looking bewildered, and then
scurry off under the bushes. If Carol and I had to work that hard,
I'm not sure we would have had kids. Our "work," though, is not

only physical but also emotional and psychological, even spiritual, because human brains are more complex and nuanced.

As I watch the mating squirrels, I can't help but wonder about my romantic vision of the Towhee-Cardinal family a few months ago. Perhaps a lover of birds just wants to believe that birds can love. And I'm not fond of squirrels. I spend more time trying to run them out of the bird feeders than feeding the birds. So what I see in their wild antics this morning is pure physical instinct—sex without love. Which also has its appeal: The male squirrel doesn't have to articulate how he feels about his mate or where he thinks their relationship is going. And the female doesn't have to interpret the emotional implications of all his nutty, self-absorbed twitters. Color and smell and size and physical aggression—testosterone—overwhelm a tiny sliver of reason. This is probably why squirrels and chipmunks mate pretty much the same way they always have.

We are the only species that understands sex as an expression of love, the only animal that "makes love." And we make it for an infinite variety of reasons. Some people still "do it" merely for the purposes of reproduction, but most don't. Our species has devastated the environment in the last fifty years, and so the planet simply can't withstand the continued growth of *Homo sapiens*. Some people have sex both for pleasure and to physically/emotionally reinforce a loving, committed relationship. Others have sex for pleasure alone—without strings, or commitments, as friends with benefits.

Since I was a kid in the sixties, our culture has become much more open about human sexuality. And that's a good thing. Tessa and her friends seem to know as much about sex by their first year in high school as I did as a freshman in college. They've had a better education, but it's also due to a new reality: sex permeates our culture. More is never enough. Sexual language and imagery scream from every billboard and TV and computer and cell phone screen—from Internet newsfeeds to pop-up ads. According to a recent Kaiser Foundation study, 80 percent of teenagers' favorite

TV shows include overt sexual content, and a third include sexual behavior. I don't think this is so terrible. But the constant sexual bombardment and the focus on physical perfection can confuse children and adolescents. They may not know that perfection is not about flawlessness but about wholeness. Nor that sex, as wondrous as it is, is not a prerequisite for falling or being in love.

When I was twelve years old, I got very excited by the alluring Ginger on *Gilligan's Island* (a sixties TV sitcom). Whenever she tried to kiss Gilligan, I could feel his trembling confusion like it was my own. And I remember being intensely aroused by a then-provocative scene in the 1969 movie *Butch Cassidy and the Sundance Kid:* a bedroom encounter between Robert Redford and Katherine Ross where the camera briefly panned a tantalizing two-inch gap in an open robe between Ross's breasts. They didn't show the breasts or anything else—and certainly not the sex that I now presume followed this scene. (I had little understanding of sex at the time.) But for days after seeing the movie I squirmed with excitement and kept replaying the scene in my head. There was no videotape or DVD with which to actually watch it again though, so I had to rely on my memory and imagination. Which is my point here: much less regarding sex is left to the imagination these days. The most recent evidence: a new TV show called *Hung,* which revolves around a particular physical attribute of the main character. Now that's a show that the squirrels and chipmunks might understand.

But they've all disappeared from the yard now, so I go back inside and return to my reading—to Thoreau's *Journal.* It's a pleasant shift from *Walden,* which is often so distilled that it lacks the honesty of its source—the *Journal.* Case in point: I find a picture of an erect penis in the October 16, 1856, entry. Like all of Thoreau's doodles, it's a simple line drawing, the phallus vertical on the page, protruding from a small scrotum. The erection is floating in white space, unattached to an owner. So I cannot tell to which animal it belongs, but I suspect a human. Startled by the image, I have a wild flurry of thoughts before reading the entry.

Why had none of my professors ever mentioned this drawing, which I assume would have been scandalous in the Victorian era, when sexual experience was rarely discussed and deeply repressed? After all, this was not a secret letter that had just been discovered, but part of a journal that has been in publication for over a century.[2] Could this be a self-portrait, or that of a close friend—perhaps a sketch of his walking partner Ellery Channing, or one of the many men he writes of in his *Journal*? No, I would have heard about that. What was I missing?

Quite a bit, actually. I then read the entry. The drawing is of a mushroom he has discovered near the Cambridge Turnpike. Thoreau describes "the rare and remarkable fungus" in minute detail.[3] It is six and three-quarters inches long and consists of a cap, a stem, and a base—"or a scrotum, for it is a perfect phallus." The cap has "an oblong mouth at tip measuring about one eighth of an inch long" and "defiles" what it touches "with a fetid, olivaceous, semi-liquid matter." Then, after describing the mushroom as if it were a penis dripping with semen, Thoreau calls the plant "a most disgusting object." And though he wonders, "What was nature thinking of when she made this?" he pulled a few up and brought them home with him: "In an hour or two the plant scented the whole house. . . . It smelled like a dead rat. . . ."[4]

Sigmund Freud would have had a field day with this story. He might claim that Thoreau was transferring his unexpressed love and confused sexual desires to the plant—that he was less confused by the "natural purpose" of the phallus in the woods than by what to do with his own. And though Thoreau's writing did turn away from self and more toward serious botany in the post-*Walden* period, this seems like a fair line of reasoning. None of the other detailed plant descriptions in the *Journal* are quite so negative. None "defile" whatever they touch.

This reading of Thoreau's mushroom discovery also makes some sense given his wider life and the sexual repression of the era. At twenty-one, Thoreau fell in love with and proposed to

Ellen Sewell, and was rejected. He dearly loved his brother John, who tragically died from tetanus at twenty-six.[5] He was close to his mother and to his sisters—Helen, and particularly Sophia. He was fond of Emerson's wife, Lydian, and more so of Emerson's aunt, Mary: he lauds her "masculine appreciation of poetry."[6] The women he was attracted to were older, intellectual, and unavailable. In his early thirties, he wrote about a party he attended that he clearly didn't enjoy: ". . . I derive no pleasure from talking with a young woman simply because she has regular features. The society of young women is the most unprofitable I have ever tried."[7]

You don't have to read all his books or all of the *Journal* to figure out that Thoreau seems more drawn to men. Like his contemporary, Walt Whitman, Thoreau lived at a time when being gay was quite risky, and when terms like "sexual identity" or "sexual orientation" didn't exist.[8] But unlike Whitman, he never explored his sexuality in print.[9] Rather, he devoutly defended physical purity and chastity.[10] Whitman's sexual directness may have both attracted and confused Thoreau, and may have revealed to him the one area of self-understanding where he was deficient.

And so it is possible that Thoreau's greatest physical intimacy and pleasure may have come from lying in some cool, wet weeds, or tasting a sour apple in the woods, or plunging naked and alone into the cold, deep water of the pond. In retrospect, this all could seem rather sad. But on the other hand, his redirected passions and desires may be the source of his genius, of his rare ability to participate in the nonhuman natural world, in the life of ants and owls. He writes openly of this Wild love: "How rarely a man's love for nature becomes a ruling principle with him like a youth's affection for a maiden, but more enduring! All nature is my bride."[11]

After tiring of Thoreau's sex life, or lack thereof, I walk over to the Glen Ellyn library to consult a mushroom guidebook and see whether the thing actually exists. It does: *Phallus ravenelli*. It is part of a family of mushrooms called stinkhorns and emits the strong odor of rotting flesh. The photo in the guide looks like Thoreau's drawing in the *Journal*. And the one place they mention it is common (this is a national guide, not a state one) is southern Michigan. I've never seen one in my spring trampings around the cabin, but then I wasn't looking for it.

I put the guidebook back and use a library computer to check my e-mail. For some reason the spam filter has not been working on my account, and thus junk e-mail has been flowing freely to my in-box. In the last week I have received hundreds of e-mails about working from home, lowering insurance rates, getting out of debt, or obtaining an online degree, or a designer watch, or cheap Valium, or a free trip to the Bahamas—everything someone presumes I need or want.

If these subjects are a kind of loose barometer of the American psyche, I wonder what Thoreau would think about the most common topic amid this scroll of e-mails. The majority of them concern cheap Viagra and penis enlargement. The subject lines are amusing: "Tablet of happiness," "Real men, real tools," "Make your buddies envious," and the one that just arrived as I'm writing: "I wonder why you're still shy." I open it: "Attain average girth increase by 20% and add 2–3 inches to length in one month without any difficulties! You can trust this method, as it is absolutely natural."

What would Thoreau have thought of such ads, of such openness? He might smile at the word *natural* and critique the crass marketing. But if he listened and looked around, and absorbed the comfort that people now have with their sexuality, he might also appreciate the possibilities and open up a bit, perhaps letting his eyes rise up from the ground, to see and talk with young, attractive women—and with men, who he might now find attractive in mind *and* body.

But my guess is that in spite of his seeming lack of experience, Thoreau would also critique our modern perceptions of sexuality. He might be a bit puzzled by how far we haven't come, by our new (old) obsessions and insecurities, by a hypersexualized human body whose component parts are now reduced to marketable commodities. He might wonder if anyone really believes that penis and breast enlargement will bring happiness. And he might wonder about what romance has become—why anyone would choose to meet and chat on Facebook rather than in the flesh. Or to fly with a partner to a Jamaican resort for a romantic weekend getaway, rather than walk down your own street, hand in hand in the moonlight. He might wonder why so many of us know so much about the sex lives of movie stars and professional athletes and so little about our own. He might suggest we put less energy into perfecting the marketing of sex and more into exploring the meaning of love—which, he might remind us, includes but does not always require sex.

Chapter 9

Lake Glass
Childhood and Parenthood

Objects are concealed from our view not so much because they are out of the course of our visual ray, as because we do not bring our minds and eyes to bear on them.

HENRY DAVID THOREAU[1]

We're all at the cabin for a couple of days. It's early, and no one else is up, so Bennett and I are sitting in the porch munching on cinnamon rolls, sipping orange juice, and playing Yahtzee. When I look over at him, I suddenly remember doing the same thing with my dad a long time ago in a different cabin. We modeled this cabin after that one—cabin #13 at Tower Hill Church Camp, which is about two miles from here. In the sixties, our family spent a week there every summer. The woods around #13 were kind of like these woods here at the farm—full of owls and raccoons and poison ivy. But the camp was near the water. Just beyond that green patch of woods, the dunes rolled down to the slow blue pulse of the lake.

Tower Hill was a rustic, inexpensive getaway, and because the camp staff was overworked and underpaid, a low-maintenance camp. The tennis court demanded a nuanced game. The challenge was not to keep the ball inside the lines (which were mostly worn away) but to hit a piece of the pavement that wasn't buckled or cracked, or overgrown with weeds. The playground was a heavy, splintering teeter-totter, a metal merry-go-round, and a steel slide that grew so hot in the afternoon that it would raise blisters on your legs.

The paint was always peeling on cabin #13. Mosquitoes and horseflies and yellow jackets found the small holes ripped in the porch screens. The windows, all propped open with sticks, would crash down on your fingers if you tried to close them. Mice lived in the electric oven during the winter; when you turned it on in July you were baking mouse-crap pie, filling the space with a nauseating stench. The cabin's outhouse was loaded with spiders and centipedes. At night, monster bugs lurked in the black corners, just outside the flashlight's beam.

Yet my three older brothers and I loved the place. Maybe it was the blurring of the inside and outside, or how time slowed until it moved like the clouds drifting above the woods. My favorite part of the day was the mile-long walk each morning from the cabin to Lake Michigan. The sweetness of white pine mingled with sweat and suntan lotion. The plastic rattle of sand shovels and buckets echoed each step, a rhythmic backdrop for my brothers' teasing and laughter and my parents' quiet conversations. At the end of the walk, we exited the dark woods onto the dunes in anticipation, breaking into a jog for the last one hundred yards. And then it appeared again—the unbroken promise of the lake—more water than we could ever hope for. And it went on forever. We sprinted over the sizzling sand, pranced into the cold water, and lunged into the curl of a wave.

Now, forty years later, Carol and I return with our kids here to our replica of cabin #13 and drive to that same stretch of woods and lake at Tower Hill. We walk through the same piece of the forest, the same colors and smells. And when the kids emerge from the woods onto the beach, they, too, feel the urge to run for the water. They make their mad dash, and I take off after them. My limbs don't bend as far or as fast as they once did, but I can keep up. Barefoot in the hot sand, I dive back into the lake and the shivering joy of childhood.

One summer when I was seven, I read a book about a boy in Maine who sent a letter in a bottle to a friend on the other side of the ocean. Though it never arrived, I loved the dream of the bottle drifting across the wild sea. So I decided to try it: I would send a letter to my friend Paul in Lexington, Missouri, where we lived at the time. I don't think I understood that Lexington was not on Lake Michigan. I'm not sure that I even knew that the lake was not an ocean. The Missouri River ran by Lexington, and it was big, so I figured it would work.

That very afternoon, I scribbled a short letter to Paul on a half sheet of paper, rolled it up, put a rubber band around it, and stuck it in a thick green Coke bottle I found in a trash can at the beach. I pushed the note all the way to the bottom of the bottle. For a cork, I jammed in a wet stick and broke it off near the opening. I walked a few feet into the lake and threw it in, and it splashed about ten feet from where I was standing. A calm, still day, the bottle lolled on its side and soon began to wash slowly back toward shore. I walked out and retrieved it. Some water had gurgled in, so I removed the stick, poured out the water, reinserted the stick, and threw it out further. I did this three more times, until the water was up to my neck. After the final throw, I stood in the cool green water, watching. The bottle soon disappeared, and I knew it had filled with water and sunk to the bottom. Though I couldn't understand it then, what bothered me was not just that the letter wouldn't arrive, but that I lost the story, the drifting bottle of words bobbing through storm and calm, past steamers and fishermen, toward my friend.

I still wonder what happened to the message I tried to mail to Paul in 1967. The stick and letter have long since dissolved, but what of the Coke bottle? I presume it either cracked in the water or washed in and broke on the shore. Then, over time, the glass fragments would become more hydrated and begin to soften and erode—by the hour and day and decade. The rock and sun, the undertow and riptides, the lateral tug and pull of the waves, wear the glass down. The lake tumbles our trash into treasure, broken shards into frosted gems, into lake glass.[2]

But it takes a long time—often twenty or thirty years, depending on the thickness of glass. Most of the pieces I find are brown (beer bottles) or white (soda bottles) or green (wine or beer bottles). Some are the size of my pinky fingernail, others as large as a half-dollar. Unlike the note in the bottle, these drifting fragments are a wordless story read with the palm and fingers. The most weathered, pitted pieces are the most valued. Their beauty stems from their *seasoning,* from how much of the lake's memory they carry. But if undiscovered by someone like me, they would eventually disappear, returning to their origin, to tiny bits of sand.

I have a large bowl full of lake glass on my desk. When my writing goes poorly, I pick up a piece—touch a story of loss, of transformation—and imagine the cold, deep re-membering of the lake, the constant journey of glass back to sand.

Glass and sand have been woven into one journey for thousands of years. Glass blowing originated in 250 BC, and the first U.S. glass factory was founded in New Jersey in 1739. But the recipe for glass has never changed much. Most glass today is still about 70 percent sand (silica) mixed with 15 percent soda (sodium bicarbonate) and 10 percent lime (calcium oxide), which is then superheated (2,400 degrees Fahrenheit) until it liquefies. Glass can be recycled endlessly, from glass to sand to glass and back again.

Consider what this cycle of glass and sand actually measures: the time it takes for the lake to recover from our excess, to clean up our mess. Twenty or thirty years is a short time compared to how it long it takes for rocks and stones to break down and granulate—five hundred or even a thousand years. But it is a long time compared to how quickly the lake is poisoned by human activity, by coal and nuclear and manufacturing plants, by pesticides and fertilizers and untreated sewage.[3] These poisons—mercury, furan, dioxins, PCBs, and others—are hard to see early on, when more could be done to stop their harm. Consider the birth defects of a baby whose mother has eaten too many mercury-filled salmon, or the cross-billed syndrome in cormorants, or other genetic defects in terns and frogs, or the cancerous tumors in lake trout and herring gulls and other predatory animals. We don't see this degradation until years after the dumping, and far from where the chemicals entered the water. Lake Michigan is sick. She may be able to heal, but only on her time—by the clock of sun and water and the ticking of sand in the wind.

When I told Abby about the slow process of lake glass, I mentioned that it is now also simulated by some small companies, which compress several decades of life in the lake into a few hours with chemicals and large tumblers, resulting in hundreds of pounds of imitation lake glass. The mass-produced glass is then sold for everything from jewelry to countertops to bathroom windows.

This got Abby thinking. One morning at the cabin, she made her own lake-glass factory with a quart-size plastic bottle. She put in three fistfuls of pebbles and three of sand, then added several shiny pieces of a newly broken glass and filled the bottle three-quarters full with lake water.

"I'm going to shake it for five minutes every hour," she said. Then she started shaking. On the way back to Chicago that day, I heard the sloshing rattle in the back seat every now and then. She checked the glass a day or so later but then forgot about it. I found the bottle a month later sitting in the garage, the water evaporated, the glass pieces still sharp and shiny, the mystery of time not yet unraveled.

It's good to tumble scrap glass into faux lake glass rather than dump it in landfills, but I'm also glad that genuine lake glass is distinctive. It is more frosted and pitted, while artificial glass is smoother, heavier, and too symmetrical to have been turned by the lake. Yet the fake glass looks authentic to a novice, and it's cheap if you buy it online: $8 a pound for exotic reds and blues and purples you'd never find on the beach.

But the attraction of lake glass for me is less in the finding than in the looking. "Seek and ye shall find"—not lake glass, or mushrooms, or wildflowers, but the awareness that comes from the seeking itself, and that rounds the anxious, confused edges of the seeker.

The key to finding lake glass is learning how to see it. It's like learning to see arrowheads in a riverbed, or a sparrow in a distant tree, or worry in the way a child's hands move, or relief in a stranger's eyes. Before the brain mechanically receives the image, it intuitively seeks it out. We don't just look; we look for. We see, in part, because we imagine.

On an overcast day, a penny-size shard of clear glass newly rinsed by a wave and lying alone on dark sand is hard to miss. But on a bright, sunny day, the colors meld together. So a dry, frosted quarter-size piece of brown glass lying amid some brown pebbles will be missed by most. The more you walk the shoreline at different times, and learn the shifting colors of light and shadow on the water and sand, the more you learn to see.

It also matters when and where you look. I like to look in the late morning on a two-mile stretch of beach in a state park next to Tower Hill. After a storm is best, when things have been churned up and laid out to be sorted. Though much of the timing is also just plain luck: a piece of glass long buried under a hot veil of sand may be abruptly exposed for an hour or two by the wind, or a stormy surf, before being covered up again, or swept back out into the lake.

When Carol and the kids and I stay at the cabin, we try to spend several hours at the lake each day. We swim and walk the beach. I look for lake glass. So do the kids, but they are more interested in rocks—colorful ones with holes in them for necklaces or mobiles.

There are at least ten thousand interesting rocks for each piece of lake glass; rocks require less focus. But last summer, on the last day of a weeklong trip, Tessa found a large, rare shard of blue-green glass—the most beautiful piece I've ever seen. Grinning widely, she offered to sell it to me. Every time I asked, "How much?" her price went up. Abby and Bennett found this hilarious (and now all of a sudden were both searching for lake glass too). After an hour or so, we all found some small, clear pieces, but nothing like Tessa's. She finally loaned it to me for "writing purposes."

That night we marveled over Tessa's find and wondered how old it was. Twenty years? Thirty? It looked like a piece of one of those old green Coke bottles. Could it be? I had to tell them the story at least, and pose the possibility. Had Tessa found a piece of the Coke bottle I had thrown in the lake as a child? No one believed it possible, except me.

"It's a good story though," Carol said.

A bit hurt by this, I shifted to a defensive position: "Well, we couldn't prove it either way, could we? I mean, it's not like we can do carbon-14 testing."

"No, that's my point," she said, with her usual patience. "It's a good *story.*"

A good story. But I wanted a factual story, a *true* story. I don't want to leave readers on that narrow, shaky bridge between fact and truth, or between imagining and re-membering.

Or maybe I do. I've been wondering about this while rereading *Walden* this year. When I read it the first time in college, I expected to find factual reportage of what happened to him on a given day during his stay at the pond. But the book took eight years to write, and in the end he condensed his two years at the cabin into the illusion of one. It is not a nature journal, but an intensely literary recreation of Thoreau's intellectual and spiritual saunters at Walden, and the years surrounding it.

Thoreau always left the hyphen in *re-membering*, a reminder for modern readers that the imagination is not a part of memory, but a *means* of memory, of art, of putting the pieces of the story back together, of constructing truth and beauty. He creates *Walden* from matters of fact and mystery, from the measurable and immeasurable, the seen and unseen. "The imagination never forgets, it is a re-membering," Thoreau once wrote in a letter to a devotee. "It is not foundationless, but most reasonable, and it alone uses all the knowledge of the intellect."[4]

Perhaps the mind, then, is like a piece of unfinished or half-cured lake glass—partly transparent and partly opaque. If you hold the glass up to your eye and look back out at the world of the past, you can see some key details on the other side, but not all of them. The past is often cloudy. Yet the whole piece of glass can let the powerful light of memory back through on this world, throwing the here and now, the present, into a surprising clarity. To discern how the light of the past illuminates the present is the work of the imagination.

I had never even considered the possibility of finding a piece of that forty-year-old Coke bottle until Tessa made her discovery. But I had imagined another true story—that most of that glass had re-turned to sand by now, had been re-membered by the lake, that we were all walking on the bottle I had tried to send to Paul, that my childhood physically converges with my children's on that stretch of beach.

Maybe that's why I can so easily still see my parents on the same bit of shoreline—in their mid-forties, like Carol and me. And next to them is a chubby little boy with an odd, uneven haircut and large ears. I am slapping the side of a plastic bucket packed with wet sand, loosening the castle. It slides out onto the beach like a little cake, which I try to get my older brothers to notice. When they don't, I start to cry. My mom hears it above the whoosh of wind and wave. She comes over and helps me build a little moat with a shovel. We pretend the sticks are people, the sand beetles little monsters.

No one loved that bit of lakeshore more than my mom. She is eighty-six now and has not been back to that beach for many years. Eighty-six years is a long time—three times as long as it took for that piece of Coke bottle to roll up on the surf and find my daughter. But the story doesn't end. I pick the lovely blue-green piece of glass out of my bowl. Rough and round and cool in my palm, it somehow still re-members my childhood, and my children, and my mother: in her floppy hat, sunbathing on a long towel, or searching for rocks, or swimming out into the cool swell of the lake. I can see her treading in the shimmering green water with us on one of those blazing summer days so many years ago—laughing and talking and dreaming. And I wonder if she felt the same way with us that I do now when bobbing in the lake with our kids—relieved, reborn, thankful to surrender to the water and sunlight, part of both a timeless belonging and a slow wearing away.

Chapter 10

A Box of Wind
Nature and Religion

The morning wind forever blows, the poem of creation
is uninterrupted; but few are the ears that hear it.

HENRY DAVID THOREAU, *Walden*[1]

Midmorning. I have come to the cabin for an overnight, and sit
reading *Walden* as a cold rain slants into the weeds. The long, winding stream of words sparkles with insight, but after riding the raft
of Thoreau's consciousness for several hours, I lose track of where
it's going. I know that's the point—the journey matters, not the
destination—but the woodstove is blazing, and I'm getting sleepy.
I've been on page 166 for a long time: "Every man has to learn
the points of compass again as often as he wakes, whether from
sleep or any abstraction. Not till we are lost, in other words not till
we have lost the world, do we begin to find ourselves, and realize
where we are and the infinite extent of our relations."

A while later I startle awake to my own snoring. Too groggy
to "find myself," or the world Thoreau describes, I turn the tran-
sistor radio on and crank the volume. The dictatorial tone and
good-versus-evil worldview rises from a conservative Christian
station. The speaker, a Baptist pastor from Kansas, says he is go-

ing to explain the difference between spirituality and religion. After a prayer, he launches into his talk. He says that religion is like the Ten Commandments—all rules and doctrine. Spirituality, on the other hand, is how one applies this doctrine to life, how religion is lived. This seems logical but insufficient. The preacher starts in on one of the commandments, on not committing adultery and what "God requires." But he never gets to the spiritual applications, so I switch him off.

My attention abruptly shifts to the window: a cottonwood branch near the cabin cracks in the wind and falls vertically, sticking upright in the soft mud like a staff dropped from the heavens by some lost prophet. I keep watching, wondering whether I will ever see the wind spear the ground again. As the tree shakes and its leaves rise in a swirl, I consider the mystery of the wind, how it is silent and invisible except when it touches the world—snapping off dead limbs or cooling wet skin. Yesterday I woke to the low, teetering whistle of an empty beer bottle I left on the cabin steps. Though I couldn't see the bottle, I recognized the eerie, shifting tones from my youth and from my recent attempts to show Bennett how to make a bottle "sing."

This morning, as the wind swirls, I imagine Bennett running across the meadow in front of the cabin, pulling a kite into the sky. Like most kids, I too loved kites—the miracle of the wind made visible. In our little town a paper kite cost fifty cents at the Ben Franklin dime store down the street: two thin strips of wood formed a rigid, fragile cross that stretched a yellow paper diamond out to two by three feet. I tied a strip of a shirt rag on for a tail, tied the string to the point where the sticks crossed, grabbed the string at a four-foot lead, and took off running across a large field near our house. As the wind filled the paper diamond and lifted it skyward, I bailed out more string. I ran and bailed until the kite assumed a power of its own, lifted itself out of my hands, and was held aloft by something far above me.

The string unraveling in my hand measured my belief in the resilience of the kite. The more line I let out, the more I risked to the raw power of the wind. Sometimes the kite kept rising until it had pulled out the entire spool—more than a thousand feet. When I came to the end, I tied the kite to a fence post and watched the tiny yellow diamond, barely visible in the blue abyss, describe the wind. Sometimes it was too much and the string snapped, setting the kite free. No longer bound to the earth, the kite then rose for a second before zagging to the ground. I always half expected it to keep rising, like a helium balloon, like a miracle, like nature *defied*. I was disappointed to later learn that the falling kite and rising balloon instead *defined* nature, that their movements could be explained by science, by numbers.

Some older boys flew kites in that same field. One day a boy brought a new kind of kite. Rather than a paper shield that easily caught and held the wind, this kite had a rectangular box frame— two feet wide by four feet long. Made from strips of wood a bit thicker than on my kite, his had eight-inch-wide pieces of green paper wrapped around the top and bottom. The rest of the kite was open. How would this ever fly? I thought it would be too heavy, or that a gust of wind would get trapped inside and rip the paper to shreds. Off the boy sprinted with the box kite trailing behind him. After thirty yards, it rose steadily into the air. It didn't lift as easily or as quickly as my kites, but once aloft, it was more stable.

This image of the box kite—of a rigid frame that can hold and ride the wind precisely because it is open—gets me thinking about that radio preacher, about the "box" of religion, and the spirit that carries it. The Latin root of the word *religion* means "to bind together again," while the root of *spirit* means "wind or breath."

Perhaps because I'm reading Thoreau, and know of his love of etymology, I'm curious about these words. Can the spirit of meaning that writers both evoke and live in also be a part of a religion—a story or experience that "binds us together again"? Or is the religious a kind of binding of a writer's intellect and imagination? Spirit is natural, of nature. Religion is not. It is human made. Like the kite, it too is a fragile structure lifted into a journey by a force over which it has no control, yet which it can respond to and describe. So I'm left wondering: at a time when spirituality seems increasingly romanticized and vague, and religion seems dangerously closed and rigid, is it naïve to believe that they could take flight together, to imagine that they are *bound to be freed?*

Sometimes Thoreau seemed to hope they could be. He studied and wrote of the religious traditions from both East and West: "It would be worthy of the age to print together the collected Scriptures of the Sacred Writings of the several nations, the Chinese, the Hindus, the Persians, the Hebrews, and others, as the Scripture of mankind." He believed such a collection "might help to liberalize the faith of men."[2] In the end, he rejected not the spirit of religion but the spiritlessness of the institution, of many churches—of the beautiful, ornate boxes that the wind could not penetrate nor lift into mystery. "What is religion?" he once wrote. "That which cannot be spoken."[3]

※

Last month I was reminded of Thoreau's struggle to capture the religious in language, to box the wind, when I went to the Concord Public Library to read the original manuscript of "Walking," his most frequently delivered lecture. He revised the last version of the essay on his deathbed in 1862 for the *Atlantic Monthly.*

The first thing I noticed was a paragraph he scratched out and didn't include in the published version. It points to what the kite maker often lacks—a sense of reverence for what the wind can do and has always done[4]: "The trees do not brag. I have seen a pine tree in the wind sowing the seeds of a future forest which perchance would cover acres of ground for centuries to come. Yet

I have heard no other herald of this deed than the sough of that same wind through its boughs. The planting was achieved in a single gale, and no man was notified of it."[5]

My next discovery was less overt. Amid the wild, looping scrawl of his handwriting, I could not help but notice his uncertainty over when to capitalize words or ideas I assume he hoped to equate with the divine, with something bigger. In one spot he goes back and capitalizes the word *god*, which he had first written in lowercase. And in several other spots, he adds three little extension lines to the *w* in *wildness*, making them capitals, unsure how to render this central idea in his work. The same confusion appears between *nature* and *Nature*.

I left the library wondering whether the seeming contradiction of his capitalization, of first making the word *God* ordinary (*god*) and the word *nature* extraordinary (*Nature*), was arbitrary or a glimpse into the depth of Thoreau's honesty at the end of his short life. As the first celebrated American nature writer, he lived before it was a cliché to say, "The ordinary is sacred." And he understood that the word *ordinary* has religious roots (i.e., *ordination*)—that it refers to the order of a religious service. But increasingly, Thoreau found his religion in the woods themselves, in the wild, divine patterns and relationships among flora and fauna. Thus, he was finally ordained not by the Unitarians but by the sun filtering through the trees each morning.

"Nature," Emerson's renowned essay, may be the clearest early depiction of Thoreau's "religion," of how he first came to understand the Concord woods as both scripture and temple.[6] "The happiest man," Emerson writes, "is he who learns from nature the lesson of worship."[7] Unlike some, Thoreau sought no human structure or contrivance or community to worship what he called God. Not surprisingly, he finds God in the most ordinary aspects of life; his daily bath in Walden Pond is a "religious exercise." *Walden* itself sometimes feels like one long, meandering prayer of discovery and gratitude. When the tone shifts to moments of frustration or impatience, it is usually due to the most confounding animal of all—the kite maker, the wind boxer.

ॐ

Early afternoon. The rain has stopped, and the sky has cleared. I walk from the cabin to the farmhouse to get some coffee. When I emerge from the shady woods, the sun is flooding the farmyard. A gust of wind blows through a row of old silver maple trees. And then this: the cool air alive with the golden rain of a thousand spinning seeds. The maple-copters have taken flight.

Another gust and another flock of the twirling blades of sunlight is cast out and hovers down around me. I feel a bit of hope, or maybe it is faith. In what, I'm not sure, but I think it is in the wind and what the wind can do. What I know is that the warm balm of sunlight has turned the blowing rain of seeds into a moment that doesn't end, a shimmering presence.

I lie down on an old cedar picnic table underneath the trees. The maple-seed shadows, the whirlybird silhouettes falling across the barren wood, are as magical as the seeds that are landing on my body and in the tangle of my hair. Below me, I watch the spinning shadows in the grass, where the odd mirror of their dark revolutions ends, and a new life may begin. Then I sit down in the wet grass and try to watch the flight of one individual seed: how it spirals down, how the little propeller slices the air in tiny circles of self-suspension. But I can't do it. I lose it in the awe of the whirling multitude.

Thoreau called these seeds "maple keys." The veined seed and blade do vaguely resemble a house key, but the metaphor—the either-or, locked-unlocked connotation—never fit for me. This afternoon, however, something feels different. The cool breeze has blown up into a surprising gale, and I, too, long to be carried in new directions, to be lost, even in a familiar landscape.

When the wind frees another cloud of the winged yellow seeds, I feel something opening in me. I try to assign a word to this un-locked moment, but none really work, whether capitalized or not. So finally, I just let go, and fall into the great current of wonder, trusting that the quiet faith of a maple tree and a thousand whirl-ing prayers will carry me home.

AUTUMN

October is the month for painted leaves.
Their rich glow now flashes around the world.
As fruits and leaves and the day itself
acquire a bright tint just before they fall,
so the year near its setting.

HENRY DAVID THOREAU[1]

Chapter 11

Trimming Trees
Self-Reliance and Self-Destruction

A man is rich in proportion to the number
of things which he can afford to let alone.

HENRY DAVID THOREAU, *Walden*[1]

A lone nuthatch perches on the wooden lip of our bird feeder and scratches at the seed. I sit on the back porch watching him, drinking coffee, and surveying our yard. Tomorrow the village of Glen Ellyn will pick up and haul away tree branches free, so I've got a project in mind—a "forest management" project. It's a bit out of my handyman comfort zone, but I'm determined.

The problem is the forty or so Asian elms and the few mulberries that frame our yard. Some arborists call them junk trees because they're brittle and messy and drab in autumn. You might say they're the opposite of a sugar maple or a red oak. Nobody plants them on purpose anymore. Our neighbors tell us the elms were planted forty years and two owners ago as a hedge. But no one ever trimmed it, so they didn't have enough space or light and grew into a scraggly fifty-foot-high border fence. Now it sways in the wind like a line of tattered old paintbrushes that have lost their shape and can no longer hold any color.

Or maybe not. Carol doesn't see them that way. She watches the treetops drift to and fro against the summer sky and sees a stubborn beauty, and the homes of dozens of animals—birds and squirrels and raccoons and possums. "There's no such thing as a junky tree," she says.

I see her point. And I agree that habitat is important. And maybe *junky* is the wrong adjective. But they *are* high-maintenance trees. I don't mind the elm limbs that crack in the wind and fall in our yard every few days, because I can saw them up for firewood. But the mulberry trees get on my nerves this time of year. By late August the whole yard smells like a vat of fermented fruit. And all the gutters are literally "jammed." I've considered squatting over the downspout with toast and a knife some morning just to startle the neighbors.

This summer the elms and mulberries grew at their typical rate—like *weeds*—five or six feet at the crown. And the mid-level branching was denser than we could ever remember. The formidable green wall formed a nice privacy fence we enjoyed for most of the season. But then one day, as the leaves began to fall and I was poking around the house looking for spots to scrape and paint, I happened to look up and notice something I should have noticed long ago: an elm tree growing into our second-story roof vents. And worse, a large mulberry was growing into our chimney and over the main power line. Not good. Even Carol agreed that the mulberry was a problem.

I spent the next few days getting estimates for tree removal. But when the weekend came, and Carol and the kids left on an overnight trip to visit friends, for some reason my thrifty, small-town Iowa brain started clicking. I got another idea: rather than pay the "tree-care professionals" $1,500 to trim the elms and cut down the mulberry, I would do it myself.

After all, I thought, I've been reading Thoreau for almost a year: Mr. Simplify. Mr. Self-Reliance. Mr. If-I-Can't-Do-It-It-Needn't-Be-Done. What had I learned from my study that was useful? I wasn't sure. Though I knew that the blind reverence I had in college for Thoreau's minimalism had shifted. Now his "Simplify" philosophy seemed less political and more practical. He didn't live on water and beans and berries and build his little cabin from a recycled shanty for the good of nature, or for some greater common good. His reasons were more honest, and practical: he sought to free himself from economic need, and thus from labor. This approach would ensure his leisure—the freedom to write and walk and think. He sought just enough food and clothing and shelter to achieve this kind of freedom.

Though I also long for such freedom, Thoreau's method doesn't work for me. I'm minimally skilled and slow at such jobs, so it makes more sense to hire others to do the work while I teach more to pay for it. And, unlike Thoreau, I could never whittle my expenses and my work and familial responsibilities down to almost zero. His *enough* isn't nearly enough for me.

Yet I still feel a distant connection to that do-it-yourself approach. Even though I earn my keep by encouraging college students to write good papers and read good books—mostly indoor activities—I often long to be working outside with my hands. Maybe it stems from my childhood—from baling hay, walking beans, and pruning apple trees. I still crave that physical connection to the natural world, which is why I'm taking on the tree project. To trim or fell a tree is to learn how it branches and flowers and spreads its seed, and how it smells inside and out—its skin and blood, the bark and sap. It's intimate. The problem is, in the case of the mulberry anyway, it can also be dangerous.

But I'm getting ahead of myself. Before I get on with the tree cutting, I should mention that this is not my first venture into suburban self-reliance. Neither a highly skilled handyman nor a dabbling novice, in the last few years I have resolved quite a few yard and house dilemmas. (The word *re-solve* matters here, as I usually don't solve it on the first try.) But admittedly, I sometimes bite off more than I can chew. I try to forget about those endeavors as quickly as I can. But Carol remembers. Which is why I'm doing the trees today. If she were here, she would see this project as a disaster approaching in the rearview mirror in slow motion. "Do you really need to do this today?" she'd ask. Which would lead to a lengthy discussion and eventually to common sense—to hiring the job done.

But she's not here. So I drive to the hardware store and buy an electric chain saw for $89 and a hundred-foot-long bright orange extension cord. When I get home, I put on my bicycle helmet, wrestle our thirty-foot fiberglass ladder out of the garage, and try to set it up against the first elm. It's heavy, and for a brief moment the ladder takes control. But I regain it and set it in a stable position. Then I go inside, plug in the extension cord near the piano in the family room, thread the other end of the cord through a window, go back outside, plug in the chain saw to the extension cord, climb up the ladder, turn on the saw, and go to work. Though the cord keeps winding itself around the ladder and my feet, and I keep *almost* falling twenty-five feet with a roaring chain saw in my hands, I avoid catastrophe and manage to do a pretty good job trimming the elms. And this somehow emboldens me to take on a more difficult challenge: the mulberry in the power line.

The devil mulberry is near the front corner of the house. I call my friend Jim to come over and help. He brings a long rope with him, which he ties to several high crotches in the tree in order to pull it down after I cut through it at the base. I make a V notch on the away side so it will fall away from the house. Jim pulls the rope taut as I begin to cut, getting ready to guide the tree out of the power line. But as soon as I have sawed three-quarters through the tree, it starts to fall the wrong way—back into the power line. The top half of the tree is so twisted and heavy that the notch doesn't work. Jim tries like crazy to pull it back, but the tree is too big: maybe thirty feet tall with a twenty-inch girth— a lot of weight.

Now the entire tree is hung up, dangling from the electric line and chimney. And the base of the tree, which I have just cut through, is hovering about a foot above the ground. This is the first time I fully appreciate why those big, dead limbs dangling from big trees are called widowmakers—they can kill you.

It is at this moment that a squirrel darts onto a brick just below the swaying trunk, perhaps drawn by the moving shadow. He stands on his back legs and puts both of his little squirrel hands on the tree as if he is trying to steady it for me—clearly unaware that he's flirting with a medieval execution. "No!" I say. "Get out of there!" My stomach sinks. If squirrels are curious, what about the neighborhood kids? I scan the area for our neighbors and anyone else who might be wandering by. I look for Jim but can't see him.

The squirrel darts away, and the trunk stills. But I have to get the weight off the damn power line. We have just upgraded to 200-amp service. This is bad. Convinced that the tree will either fall and kill someone or rip down the power line and electrocute them, I race inside with the chain saw and extension cord and up to our second-floor bedroom. I open the window to find the massive tree suspended just two feet from the sill. If I can cut through the trunk up high and drop it straight below, I can get most of the weight off the power line and the chimney and avert disaster.

So, without thinking that the tree itself might be carrying an electric charge, I push our bed and nightstand out of the way, plug the saw in, and lean out the open window to try to cut through the dangling mulberry. Other than the chips and sawdust flying into our bedroom, the first half of the cutting through the trunk goes well. But then the saw starts to bind, and the tree begins to sway. I hold tight to the saw, but the demonic tree nearly pulls me out the window—onto the electric line. I do the only thing I can. I let go.

This is when Jim appears below me on the ground and looks up in dismay to see a large tree with a chain saw stuck in it tangled in a power line—and me, leaning out our bedroom window trying to both wrestle the saw back from the tree and keep the extension cord from wrapping around my arms. I start to feel guilty for pulling Jim into my little nightmare.

"I'll get it out!" I yell down. "Don't worry!"

And with a little luck, and five long minutes of pulling and twisting and swearing, I do get the saw out. Then I cut a new V on the other side and finally get all the way through the trunk. The tree hits with a thud I can feel on the second floor and then falls against the house, breaking a piece of siding and missing our picture window by a foot. With the weight gone, the taut power line goes slack. Success. I pull the remaining mulberry branches off the line and the chimney and drop them on the ground.

Carol and the girls got home a few hours later and walked around the yard and the scattered piles of limbs and stumps with their mouths hanging open. Bennett thought it was cool and the girls were amused, but Carol was pissed. I didn't tell her the whole story until that evening. That was when she walked into the bedroom to unload her suitcase and saw the wood chips and smelled the chain oil, and noticed it had dripped onto the bedspread. I had closed the bedroom door and forgotten to clean up the mess. My plan had been to downplay the whole thing—to cast it in a positive (money-saving) light. Why create anger and more regret when it wasn't necessary? But Carol was already mad about the way I had trimmed the elms in back (they weren't exactly even), and so the bedroom scene simply reinforced her worst fears about my lack of common sense.

"What were you thinking?!"

I avoided slipping into an angry adolescent response, which such reprimands sometimes spark in me. Instead, I made three lengthy and circuitous attempts at explaining. Then Carol was silent for a long time. And though she again avoided saying "I told you so" throughout the whole debacle, I kind of wish she would have. Because the silence felt worse. And because she did tell me.

"Please just don't ever do that again."

"OK," I said. "I'm sorry." And I was, though at the edge of my mind I was also thinking, Well, I won't ever do *that* again. Next time I'll tie and notch the tree properly, and I'll get a real chain saw, with a gas engine, with power, so I don't have to work so hard and deal with the damn cord. Next time I'll get it right.

Chapter 12

Constructing Truth
Wood and Word

Shall we forever resign the pleasure of construction
to the carpenter?

HENRY DAVID THOREAU, *Walden*[1]

Early morning. I decide to repair the cabin stairs, which are falling apart. There is just one step and a landing, but several of the boards are bowing out, pulling away from the base. The problem may be the two-by-four posts they're attached to. They also look warped. My plan is to pry off the step and landing, dig up these posts, and replace them with treated four-by-fours.

And though I'm a little better with a circular saw than a chain saw, I'm not sure whether this will work. So I make a crude drawing and drive a few miles to a small lumberyard near Bridgman to confirm my plan with someone who knows what they're doing. Upon arriving at the lumberyard, I spot a grizzled sixtysomething man in jeans, a T-shirt, and a nail apron who is sorting through a pile of ten-foot two-by-fours. He sets one end of a board on the floor, holds the other end up to his eye, and looks down its length, then turns it to each corner and does the same thing—looks down the edge line, trying to see whether it is twisted and bent or straight and square.

I can't help but remember when I first tried to do this. I was at a Home Depot, buying studs to finish a room in our basement, when I saw a burly guy in coveralls doing it—long-eyeing a two-by-four. Too embarrassed to ask him exactly what he was looking for, I queried a young kid who worked there instead. He didn't know. He thought maybe bugs had damaged them, but he was from the garden section, so he pulled his cell phone out of his orange apron and tried to call someone who might know. No luck.

So I just acted like I knew what I was doing. It's a strategy that has served me well in the past—for everything from dating in college to giving papers at academic conferences. I picked out an eight-foot two-by-four from a huge stack and looked confidently down the edge line. At first I didn't see anything. But the next one looked kind of twisted. I eyed three more. They were all bowed—long, slow curves that would be trouble. Then I found one that seemed pretty straight and square. Then another. After fifteen minutes, I couldn't tell the best boards from the good ones, but I could identify the bad ones. I was learning how to see.

That's why now, as I watch the old guy in the nail apron at the lumberyard, I have a faint desire to pick up a board and hold it to my eye, to see how much I know. But that's not why I'm here. When I ask him about fixing the stairs, he patiently lays the stud down and turns toward me. I show him my little drawing, and he looks amused, and then concerned. He thinks my plan is OK, that the treated four-by-fours are a good idea, but that rather than buying new wood, I should use the old boards if they're not too bowed. He says I could true them with a jointer or plane.

This was more help than I was expecting. "True them?" I ask.

"Yeah," he says. "You can often restore the wood so it's square with itself."

I nodded and thanked him. I didn't say that we don't have a jointer, that I've never used one, and that every piece of wood I've ever planed by hand has always ended up a bit wacky—*untrue*—

looking like what it is: the lie of my carpentry, curiosity and persistence masquerading as skill and experience.

I appreciated the man's kind advice. Not for practical reasons—I wouldn't true the boards; that would be a disaster. I bought new boards after I was sure he had left the store. Still, he got me thinking about other things. As I drove home with my eight-foot four-by-four perilously sticking out the passenger-side window of our Honda Civic (frightening the driver of every car I passed), I could not help but marvel at the language of carpentry.

True is also a verb! That's downright Thoreauvian. And so was the man's advice, because Thoreau built his cabin from salvaged wood he bought from a railroad worker, and he was skilled with a hand plane.[2] And what better way to describe Thoreau than as a man who was square with himself. That seems like it was his central task, to true his wild inner self with the outer wild all around him. Or perhaps it was to true a sentence as well as a board, honing and shaving it, preparing it to fit tightly and securely within a paragraph, so that the whole thing would hold together and be reliable, maybe beautiful.

The difference, though, is that the truth of lumber is determined with tools and numbers, while the truth of language is a necessary mystery. Even so, both truths still evolve. Both wood and words swell and shrink and bend in response to the light and darkness—to the shifting temperatures and energies of the sun and mind. Nothing is ever fixed.

Which brings me back to the stairs. My learn-as-you-go approach is too slow. And I keep thinking about verbs instead of deck screws, about inner truth instead of the truth of a 90-degree corner. I'm one of those guys who measures twice yet kind of expects to get two numbers. They're usually close though. I tell myself that this is normal, but I know it's not. It's like I'm always working with a square that is slightly bent. Which I guess is why the boards, and the stair frame, and the earth, and my mind, can seem to shift at the last minute in unpredictable increments and directions.

❧

I stop hammering for a second and look up to see Dan Dale—my friend and one of the founders of this place—come whistling down the main path with Milagro, his happy, barky beagle. He has just arrived from Chicago to work on his garden and plant some fruit trees. We embrace, and he calls me what he always does: *compa* (short for *compañero*, or friend). Then he asks whether I need any help with the stairs. (We both know I do.) He suggests bigger screws to attach the risers and tamping in the dirt around the posts more firmly. And because he actually knows what he's doing, I concur.

This is how our communal farm works: the separate lives of the dozen or so members who use the place can overlap unexpectedly—for a walk or a meal or some work project. Not everyone is comfortable with this kind of uncertainty, or with shared ownership. Over the years, people have sometimes asked Carol and me why we joined a community in Michigan rather than just built our own little hut somewhere else. The answer is partly practical: we could never afford it alone—neither the money nor the time and responsibility. And the Covenant Farm, as it is known, offers rare opportunities for both solitude and community, depending on what each person seeks. So while others may come seeking to be together, I often come seeking to be alone, for a change from all the togetherness in my normal life in Glen Ellyn.

Of all the farm members, I know Dan the best. We first met twenty years ago at a church on Chicago's South Side. We were both seminary graduates with an interest in religion and Central America and the sanctuary movement and the social conscience of the church. Then, as now, we cared about similar things but were dissimilar people: I'm more artist than activist; Dan is more activist than artist. He still lives in the city; we moved to the 'burbs. His kids are grown; ours are all still young. He has a genius for creating community; I'm good at avoiding it.

"Want to go for a walk?" Dan asks. And off we tramp through the crunchy, golden oak leaves on a late-morning saunter. In about forty minutes, we cover everything from prairie restoration to Obama's foreign policy to our favorite yard games. We check the turtle eggs he marked along the path on the ridge above the ox-bow to see whether they have hatched and crawled up through the sand. They haven't. But the possums haven't dug them up, either. Then we stop at an old, gnarly apple tree, shake off a dozen or so small stragglers, and put them in our roomy pockets. But we each save one to munch on.

As I watch Dan's large, jaunty frame and straw hat walk ahead of me along the creek, I consider how much joy he finds in this piece of land, and how well he knows it. He could easily say, "I have traveled a great deal in Sawyer." He and his wife, Nancy, were married here long ago—shortly after the community bought the place. The wedding day was so rainy and muddy that the whole ceremony was conducted on a makeshift maze of scrap plywood so everyone wouldn't get stuck in the mud. There are pictures in an old album in the farmhouse.

This morning, as we ramble through the woods together, it strikes me that in spite of Dan's workaholism and his preference for community over solitude, something about him calls to mind a modern Thoreau. Perhaps it's because he often actually does what he believes in. Though he surely has his flaws, I admire his commitments, his stubborn refusal to compromise. A pastor at a small, vibrant urban parish, he knows how to do a bit of everything—not just preaching but also plumbing, carpentry, wiring, gardening, and canning. And, like Thoreau, he plays the flute! He is a cross between John the Baptist and Johnny Appleseed—a prophetic gardener, a missionary naturalist.

A few Sundays ago, Dan arrived at the farm with a number written on his arm—his police identification number. He had been arrested again for civil disobedience at an antiwar action on Saturday afternoon, gone to prison that night, gotten out early

Sunday morning, driven to his church to lead worship, and then come out here—from prison to pulpit to planting spinach in the garden, all in twelve hours. A true activist, the guy has about triple the energy of a normal person. And it was that energy and enthusiasm, and his willingness to teach us something about carpentry and community that led us to join the farm—a group of committed, creative people who love this piece of land.

And Dan is the reason we built the cabin—largely by convincing me that I could learn how to do things by doing them, that my hands could teach my head. Having long ago built geodesic domes and log cabins, Dan was gung ho on the project. The first thing he did was give me three how-to books, each weighing ten pounds and full of marginal notes. We talked about the design and then he made a drawing that looked like a game of tic-tac-toe: the grid design for the cement pier foundation. ("What are the *x*'s?" "That's where the holes go." "Oh.") The cabin would sit on fifteen cement piers. Then, using treated two-by-twelves, we would lay the joists out and construct the floor on top of them. I calculated the cost of the wood, the metal brackets and screws, the ninety bags of cement, and other miscellany at about $800. The alternative was to have someone grade the site and pour a foundation, which would cost $3,000. The saved cost was low-skilled labor—my specialty—the hole digging, and mixing and pouring the cement. So, though I really didn't know what I was doing, I decided to dig and mix.

We modeled the place after cabin #13 at Tower Hill. The footprint was sixteen feet wide by thirty-four feet long. The last ten of those thirty-four feet would be a porch framed in by five-foot-high sliding windows. There would be no water. A plastic commode would suffice for a toilet. Eventually, we would get electricity and a wood-burning stove.

While making the drawing, I couldn't help but notice that our ten-by-sixteen-foot porch was nearly the same size as Thoreau's entire cabin, which was ten by fifteen feet. The total cost of Thoreau's cabin was $28.12. But back then a dollar was a fair wage for a day's work. Today that would be more like $50. So, by modern standards, Thoreau might have spent around $1,500 on his cabin. We spent $16,000 on ours.

During the construction process, Dan would come and work with me for a day—get me started, answer my questions, convince me that I could do things that I couldn't—and then I'd try to keep going without him for a day or two. Here are some of my journal entries from that spring:

APRIL

The building site is in the woods on the edge of a meadow—a quarter mile from the farmhouse. After digging out a few saplings and mowing the weeds, Dan and I laid out the foundation perimeter with a ball of string and some wooden stakes. Then we located the center of each of the cement piers and marked them with sticks—our digging guides. The holes were fourteen inches in diameter and four feet deep—below the freezing line. The ground was soft from the spring rains, but full of rocks and tough pockets of clay. We each dug three holes before dark. Then Dan drove back home to Chicago.

MAY

This morning all six holes were full of water. A large white-tailed deer was drinking from one. When he saw me, he sprang away and caught his front leg in the next hole over. As he fell, he caught himself with his other front leg, going down to his knee on the grass. This movement prevented the leg he had caught from going deeper and snapping. At that moment, buckled on the ground, he turned his head to look at me, and I read terror in his eye. Did he think the holes were traps and that now I was moving in for the kill? I stayed still. Then he clumsily pulled his leg out of the hole, stumbled around, and pranced away. Thankfully, he missed the other holes on his way to the woods. I hadn't thought the holes dangerous. But then I checked the others and found two mice, a mole, a dozen grasshoppers, and a praying mantis—all floating dead. The robins and blue jays, however, loved the bathing opportunity.

Later, while digging, I pulled back too hard on the spade's wooden handle and snapped it, leaving the lower half and the blade stuck in the clay. I drove to Cooney's Hardware in Sawyer and bought an unbreakable fiberglass shovel. It splintered an hour later. I dug the last five holes using only the post-hole digger. Then I checked the depth and diameter of all fifteen. Pretty close. It was getting dark when I covered the holes with some old scraps of plywood.

JUNE

Finally, Dan and I were here at the same time and could do the cement piers. By 7:00 a.m., the sun was already hot. We gathered the cardboard molds for the piers from the garage, dragged them down to the building site, fit them in the holes, and then measured, cut, and set them at the right height.

Then Dan drove the garden tractor down with a metal wagon full of eighty-pound bags of cement. We split open the bags, dumped them into the wheelbarrow, added water, mixed it up with hoes, and poured and scooped the fresh cement from the wheelbarrow into each form until it was flush with the top. We stuck pieces of rebar in the piers for tensile strength and pushed heavy metal brackets into all the piers to dry in the cement. These would hold the two-by-twelves on which we'd build the floor.

As we worked, we talked and told stories to break the monotony of the labor and forget about the blisters and the heat. We ranted about the war and global warming and health care and wondered what we could do about it. We marveled that our wives could endure us, that our children loved us, and that we could spend a few days alone in the woods building a cabin. And then we turned pragmatic and wondered if Rosie's would still be open when we were finished, and if they would still grill onions for our burgers.

After eighty-three bags of cement and ten hours of talking and mixing and pouring, darkness fell, along with great, whining clouds of mosquitoes. We were exhausted, and happy. Slathered in sweat and spattered with cement, I looked up at Dan: "Hey, we're doing it—we're building a freaking cabin!" We broke into laughter. I was thankful—that we had finished all but two piers, but also for the simple pleasure of physical labor, of working all day with a friend in the sun.

After cleaning the tools, we took showers and went to the only place open at 10:00 p.m.—the local truck stop. We got root beer and chicken-fried steaks and french fries and whatever else they still had lying around to microwave. It tasted great with a lot of ketchup. The manager looked delighted that we were eating up all the food he was about to throw away. It was 11:00 when we wiped our plates clean with the last of the fries.

⁊⁊

Later that summer, Dan and I finished laying the cabin floor, but it was the following spring before the walls went up and the roof was on. That was after a friend suggested a carpenter. With his brother and their sons, they framed and roofed the place in five days, work that would have likely taken us another year of piecemeal efforts. A month later, my brother and his wife came up for a weekend and showed us how to wire the place. (Though it was a solid year before we trenched a line to the farmhouse and got the power on.) A few weeks after that, we had an insulation-and-drywall party, and with the help of other farm members got the work done. Then Dan showed me how to trim a window and a door. I finished the others—all fifteen—and learned more about the relativity of squareness and truth (how a power miter saw could compensate for my errors and mismeasurings). Then Carol and I stained the outside and painted the inside, and I added cedar baseboard and molding and laid a simple tile floor. And we were done. Or done enough. The cabin is a work in progress—there is always more to do, always a need for revision.

᳇

I'd lost touch with Dan for several months before today, so it is good to see him and to catch up. But by dusk he has to return to Chicago for a meeting. I go back to the stairs—to truing things up. I'm almost done. The four-by-fours are plumb and square now, and much stronger and more stable than the old wood. I've got the lone stair step level and the landing almost level. (It's level on one end but not on the other.) But then, when I try to close the storm door, it won't—or not all the way. Great. I've fixed the landing, but now the door won't close. Soon I figure out it's not the new landing. The door is coming unscrewed from the frame. Damn. This always happens. I start to fix something, only to notice ten more things that need attention.

Then I make the mistake of inspecting the cabin for other needed repairs and easily find a half dozen: some of the light-switch plates need to be touched up with plaster; I cut the holes too big, leaving little gaps. And the three live wires we pulled for the ceiling fan (which we never bought) are still sticking out of a hole in the middle of the ceiling like the legs of some weird electric insect. I'm afraid to touch them. An ugly seam running the length of the ceiling has opened in the drywall. Maybe I forgot to tape it. It needs to be revised—remudded, sanded, primed, painted. There are other cracks too—near a window. But those seams *were* taped.

What's happening here? Why does everything seem to be cracking and coming apart? Perhaps it's the same as with our old house in Glen Ellyn. Maybe the cabin is also settling, yielding to the clay and sand below it, to groundwater and gravity, finding the place it belongs, making itself at home. *Settling.* What a strange word that is. I wonder why it has become so negative, connoting mediocrity, or a lack of imagination, or a betrayal of one's dreams. This is the antithesis of how the early settlers, the Midwestern homesteaders, were perceived. They were fiercely independent risk takers who settled the wilderness by battling it, and by learning how to live within it. And though most of that wilderness is now gone, the challenge of settling, of adapting to one's environment—whether it be in the city or country—still remains. Most people I know are trying to settle down or settle up or settle in one way or another, trying to find a place in the world, a way to be at home where they live.

Finally, I decide to stop looking for problems and to ignore all the cracks in the drywall. I could patch them, but they might reopen, or others might open elsewhere. And Thoreau's credo has become embedded in my brain: the point is not perfection, nor arrival, nor answers, but the journey—the imperfect truth of daily life. All of which brings me back to the stairs, this simple repair job I've been puttering at all day. After one last inspection, I decide the stairs are finished. Like these sentences, they may not be true enough for some, but they are for me. And I am going to settle. So when I drive the last deck screw into the soft pine step, it is with relief and gratitude. The dark, round head of the screw is my end mark. It punctuates the end of the work, of another ordinary day, and marks the little bit of truth I was able to construct.

Chapter 13

Falling Apart
Death and Birth

How plain that death is only the phenomenon of the individual or class. Nature does not recognize it, she finds her own again under new forms without loss.

HENRY DAVID THOREAU[1]

Our cat Rosie, a gray tabby who now weighs just four pounds, is dying. She's completely deaf, nearly blind, and has been since spring. But she holds on, and we can't bring ourselves to put her to sleep. She was five weeks old when Carol and I found her at a shelter—the same week we moved to Chicago from Iowa to start our new lives together—twenty-one years ago. The kids say she's over one hundred—that a cat year equals five human years. One of my days feels like five to Rosie. The idea intrigues me. How does that work? Is cat time slower because they never worry—about what to say or wear, or if they are late to a meeting? Does Rosie have some sort of heightened kitty consciousness that allows her to live more in the present? Or maybe if I curled up in a bright square of sunlight on the oak floor for a few hours each day, those hours would begin to slow for me too, to elongate, to become something else. I wish the present would slow down.

I care for Rosie like she is an aging grandmother. I buy her gourmet food and litter: the aged-cheddar-cheese-and-albacore-tuna dry blend for seniors, and the odorless, all-natural multicat litter with "quick clumping technology." Each morning I pour some milk in a mason jar lid and take it down to her in the basement. She can no longer manage the stairs, but lately she seems to prefer the basement. Today I can't see her, but I can hear her. She makes bizarre sounds now—odd, mournful meows that sound like a baby crying. It started when she lost her hearing. No longer sneaky or surprising, she half creeps, half limps out of the shadows of my workroom toward what seems to be the highlight of her day—a few ounces of skim milk.

As much as I love this cat, I have to admit that when she goes, it won't be so terrible. Why? It's a quality-of-life issue—hers and mine. She's in physical pain. I'm not, but am concerned about hygiene. Our clothes dryer is right next to her litter box, and she has just started peeing on our clean laundry rather than in the box. I find little nuggets of poop all over the basement. It's not her fault; her body functions autonomously from her brain. Things are decaying, falling apart. It is, it seems, *her time.*

I think of this decay now, sitting outside at dusk on the back porch of our house. The wild green buzz of summer is gone. The robins and goldfinches and bluebirds have flown south or are preparing to. It is the fall. And everything falls—not just the leaves. The temperature falls as the earth again tilts away from the sun. Darkness falls more quickly as the days shorten. Plants droop and dry up and break apart. Trees fall into dormancy and stop growing. Their leaves and seeds fall into the cool air, and then to the ground, where they will rot and root and become something new. This is the season of *decay*—a word that means "to fall away"—to return to your constituent parts, to what you are made of. We die and fall apart, but the parts go on. The same is true for the human species. Though lately I'm finding how much harder it is to accept this cycle with people than it is with pets or plants—particularly if they die suddenly, and seem to fall outside of the natural cycle of time.

ॐ

Yesterday I saw our friend John at the YMCA. He lives four blocks away from us, but I know him mainly through Carol, who works with his wife, Ellen. They are both school social workers who run programs that assist new immigrant families. Ellen has cancer. She's just fifty-six, and their family is very close; she's the kind of mother you can see in her three boys. So, when I ask John, "How are you doing?" as he stands ready to get on the treadmill, it's a huge question—probably too big to have asked.

"Oh, as well as I can," he says. His eyes are exhausted and teary, and I can only presume he is running from and toward the enormous weight of loss, of losing Ellen. I wish I could think of something comforting and useful to say.

"Let us know if there's anything we can do to help." I say "us," but we both know I mean Carol, in whom I can also feel the pending loss of Ellen. Ever since Ellen called to say they were stopping radiation, and that she had perhaps two months left, Carol has been depressed and preoccupied. I imagine the questions she carries: Why is this happening? Why Ellen? What really matters anymore? How do I live in gratitude for Ellen's life, and for life in general? How long can an hour be, or a day, up against the end of a life?

Carol visited Ellen this afternoon. Tonight in bed she was writing about it in her journal. When I asked her how it had gone, she broke down. Unable to speak, she handed me the journal.

Went to see Ellen today. She's in a lot of pain. The radiation damaged her bones and joints. "I don't know when I should give up," she said. "I'm not done yet. I'm just not done. That's what John and I keep saying to each other. I have more to do. My son said he'd move up the wedding for me. I really want to see him get married. I really do. (Now we are both crying.) But I want to see him have babies, too." Then she just wailed, and John came in to see if she was OK. And then we all cried for what was coming, for what we couldn't stop.

A week later John calls us to see whether someone can come over and stay with Ellen for a couple of hours in the afternoon while he picks his son and his son's fiancé up at the airport. Ellen is near the end, but no one knows exactly how near, so her sons fly in to visit whenever they can to spend a day or two with their beloved mother. I tell John that Carol is gone, but that Abby and I can come over. Before we go, I remind Abby that Ellen is very sick.

"I remember from when they came over for dinner," she says. "She can't talk or walk very good."

When we arrive, John takes us into the living room, where Ellen is sleeping on a foldout sofa. "I don't know if she'll wake up while you're here," he says, "but here's some water and a Popsicle if she wants it." He gives us his cell phone number. Then he kisses her, says, "I love you." Her eyes open to these words. She's groggy, but John explains clearly and gently, "Tom and Abby are here with you until I get back from the airport if you need anything." "Who?" "Tom. *Carol's* Tom, and Abby." "Oh. OK," she says faintly, in her low voice, which is a bit slurred now. Then Abby greets Ellen, but she doesn't seem to notice. John sets Abby up on a nearby computer with a blinking, beeping video game and then is off to the airport. I sit down in a chair next to the sofa bed.

Ellen has always had a striking presence; she is the kind of person in whom you sense compassion even before they speak. But I barely recognize her now. Her long, silver-brown hair is gone, and her bald head is only partly covered by a bandana above her emaciated body. I'm taken aback by all that has fallen away. Yet also keenly aware of her spirit, of her presence.

She stays awake after John leaves. I feel awkward sitting next to a woman I admire but don't know well enough for a sacred moment like this—and when she is completely vulnerable. So I ask a sequence of dumb questions, including, "How are you doing?" At this she starts coughing, so I ask if she wants some water. She says yes and raises her right arm to show she wants to sit up. I try to support her back, but she grimaces whenever she moves her gaunt body. Finally, I get her sitting up with her feet over the side of the bed. There is no back support, and no position that feels good, so she kind of leans/falls over against me—shoulder to shoulder. Her weight is slight.

"I think I need to lean on you," she says, "Is that OK?" And for the first time I hear *Ellen,* the humor, the presence. She is comforting *me* in my awkwardness.

"Yeah," I say smiling. "I think I can handle that." I give her a cup of water with a lid and a straw. She takes some sips, gives it back, and looks up at me for a second. The spirit of humor, of fun, is suddenly gone. Her dark eyes seem to carry some deep but unwelcome wisdom—the acceptance of the unacceptable.

Then she starts coughing again, which worries me, because even the small coughs shake her whole body, and seem to hurt her. I hold out the water, and she takes a few more sips and the coughing stops.

"Don't tell them about the coughing," she says. "They worry about everything." She leans back into my shoulder. Her head hangs down, her gaze falling to the carpet. "How sad that we don't see the miracle in these little things," she says in a gravelly whisper. "The little things aren't little."

I don't know whether she is talking about the water, or the carpet, or just being alive. But I can sense the dark spiral of her sadness, of loss, of time itself—how her seconds and minutes and hours are no longer numbers hurriedly scribbled in a datebook but the whole living, loving, and breathing world—the one that was/ is always here, but which she will leave. The littlest things: the delight or sorrow in her sons' eyes, the eternal rhythm of the ocean at her favorite seashore, or the wonder of an evening walk with John through this very ordinary neighborhood. The littlest things aren't little: warm air, cool water, human touch.

Ellen and I just sit there for a while leaning on each other, with the beeping electronic music of the computer game in the background.

"Is she doing OK?" Ellen asks, now suddenly aware of Abby.

"Yeah, she's fine," I say. Abby looks over and smiles.

A few minutes later Ellen says she has to go to the bathroom, which I wasn't prepared for. Facing her on the sofa, I lean over and lift her under both arms. She grabs the back of my arms and pulls. She is light and fragile when I lift her to her feet, but all of her joints hurt, so she exhales loudly and groans. Immediately sensing my worry, she says, "I'm OK" before I can ask. And then she looks up at me, and somehow we both recognize that we are in a dance position, as if, in spite of her weakness, we are about to cha-cha across the kitchen. Maybe it's because last year, Ellen, John, Carol, and I all went square dancing together. I'm not sure. But we both recognize the absurdity of the moment.

"You lead," she finally says, a sparkle of light flickering back up in her eyes. We are each grasping each others' forearms, though I'm lifting and she's leaning.

"Do you know the box step?" I ask.

"Yep," she says. She can't smile like she used to, but I can hear it in her voice—a lightness. And then we shuffle-slide across the kitchen tiles in tiny increments. It takes four or five long minutes to go fifteen feet. But we finally make it. I close the door. Ten minutes later, when she opens the door, we resume our dance position and slowly waltz back to the sofa, where she lies down, exhausted.

❧

Today I find Rosie in the basement with two feet in the litter box and two feet out. She can't lift any of her legs to move in either direction. She may have been standing like that for an hour. Her fur is dirty and matted because she can no longer clean herself. And she's shaking. I put my hand on her back: "Oh Rosie, this just isn't fair." She turns her head toward me and tries to purr, but it comes out garbled and high pitched, like a sound some other animal makes—maybe a guinea pig. I pick Rosie up, clean off the clumps of urine-soaked litter that stick to her feet and legs, and lay her on her rug. Carol and I have known this cat for half our lives, and so I'm convinced that Rosie understands my sympathy, that she draws comfort from my voice.

After work that day, I run home, pick Rosie up, and take her to the local vet. I've never been there before, so I'm at first startled by a beautifully framed 3-by-3-foot family portrait hanging on the wall by the front desk. It's a family of wheaten terriers—a close-up of their heads and shoulders with the Rocky Mountains as a backdrop. I imagine the photographer with his tripod trying to get the dogs to sit still, to pose them in that setting against their desire to be sniffing out rabbits. One of the dogs—perhaps the father—actually seems to be smiling.

When the doctor examines Rosie, he finds cataracts, a urinary-tract infection, and more infection (and perhaps tumors) in her lungs. He says she is in much pain, and that putting her to sleep is a "reasonable and humane" option. I put Rosie back in the little cardboard carrier and talk with the secretary about our options.

"We offer euthanasia by injection and cremation," she says, and hands me a price list:

$210: Private cremation. Rosie's body would be burned separately. All the ashes would be hers.

$170: Semiprivate cremation. Rosie would be burned with other animals, whose bodies would be divided only by a few bricks. Rosie's ashes would be mixed with those of the dachshund or dalmatian that were burned alongside her.

$85: Euthanasia only, and they dispose of the body.

$65: Euthanasia, and you keep the body.

We choose the low-budget option and tell the kids. They're sad, but because they've watched Rosie's decline, they also seem to have known this day was coming.

"What do you mean, 'Put her to sleep'?" Bennett asks. "I thought she was going to die."

"You're right, she is," Carol says. "It's not really sleep; it's death."

"Will it hurt her?" Abby asks.

"The doctor said that it won't. They give her a shot that puts her to sleep, but it's so strong a dose that after she's asleep for a few minutes, her heart will stop."

"And that's when she dies?" Bennett says, wanting confirmation.

"Yes. So they do 'put her to sleep,' but then she dies right after. She shouldn't feel any pain."

The next morning the kids all say their good-byes to Rosie as we make their lunches in the kitchen. Tessa brings her upstairs, cuddling her in her arms. She and Abby are crying. Finally, we get them off to school.

Early afternoon, Carol and I take Rosie to the vet. They put us in a little sterile room where we sit with the cat we love and wait to let her go. "Do you want to hold her while they do it?" Carol asks, and we both tear up. The doctor comes in. He is young and kind. "Have you had enough time to say your good-byes?" he asks. "Yes," we both say, and Carol lays Rosie on my lap. The doctor says he'll inject her with pentobarbital, a barbiturate used for anesthesia. But the dose is tripled, so Rosie will go to sleep in a minute or so, and then a minute or two later her brain and heart will stop.

Rosie seems completely relaxed and happy to be on my lap. She is purring. This stops when the vet injects her thigh, but she is oddly calm to the stick. Then the doctor leaves us alone. We both have our hands on Rosie, and can feel her breath and the soft pump of her tired old heart. We say, "I love you" again, almost as if she were a person. And then, after twenty-one years—twenty-one human years—the rhythm of her heart stops. A last breath rises and falls away, and she is dead. And I remember why *spirit* means "breath"—how the body is not all there is, even for a cat.

We lay Rosie in an orange Nike shoebox. An hour later, when the kids arrive home from school, they want to see her. I open the box, put my fingers on her belly, and can't believe she is still warm. And the way she's curled up, it's hard to believe that she's dead, that she won't wake up. It's both comforting and a little eerie. She *really* looks like she's sleeping. Bennett looks confused when he sees her. "She's dead?" he says, perhaps fearful of any surprises. "Yeah," I say. "Her blood is still warm for a little while, but she's dead. We can bury her."

"How do you know for *sure* she's dead?"

Bennett doesn't say anything, but I know he's thinking about Chip and Patch, a pair of hamsters that died last fall. It was my fault. We left town for forty-eight hours, and the weather abruptly changed. The temperature dropped from 60 down to 30. We hadn't turned the furnace on yet, and so the hamsters froze to death. We found them cold and stiff and huddled together on the floor of their cage. But when we picked them up and held them for a minute, they blinked their eyes and started to move their legs and stretch. They had come back from the dead. Like two furry little frozen batteries, the hamsters revived, their nervous systems and hearts somehow jump-started by the warmth of our hands. They died two days later, but the miracle of their resurrection, and the possibility that an animal could rise from the dead, had stuck with Bennett.

So I confirm the finality of Rosie's death. "We're absolutely sure. The doctor even checked."

"OK," he finally said, now tearing up. I pull Bennett into my arms, and he curls into my lap with his head on my chest. He rarely cuddles like this with me, and never for very long. Unless he is sick or tired, after a few seconds he is up and gone. But today he settles in, and his warm body is a comfort.

༈

I close my eyes, and my mind wanders to another dead animal and another resurrection. Tessa was just four years old. We were blissfully walking along the lakeshore on a windy summer day. In the distance a seagull rested in the sand near the water. But it was in an odd, tilted position—sort of lying on its side. After a few more steps, I could tell it was dead—a huge herring gull that didn't look to have been injured or attacked. The pristine snowy-white body glowed with sunlight; the plump, feathery breast billowed out in the wild gusts and then diminished in the calm. I tried to veer Tessa wide—away from the lake and the dead bird—by calling her attention to some cliff swallows nesting in a nearby dune. But she had already zeroed in on the gull.

"What happened?" Tessa said, clearly worried. "Why doesn't she wake up? Why doesn't she open her eyes? Why isn't she moving? Can't she fly?"

Not having prepared for the moment, I finally just blurted it out: "She's dead, honey. She died." I pretended that I knew why: she had gotten very old, and that's what happens when you get old. I mentioned *The Lion King* and the circle of life and the death of my grandfather, but these didn't satisfy Tessa's curiosity.

"Will *you* die?" she soon asked.

"Yeah," I said. "But not for a very long time."

"And Mommy, too?"

"Yes," I said. "But you shouldn't worry about it now, sweetie—"

"But how long is a long time?" she asked. I was starting to feel inadequate.

And that's when it happened. A hard, low gust of wind hit the bird from beneath and lifted its wings skyward. When the long primary feathers caught the gale, they abruptly fanned open. This sudden resistance unlocked the bird's elbows and wrists and opened the secondary feathers. In short, the beautiful, dead seagull, now animated by the wind, seemed to have become an angel in front of our eyes.

"Daddy?" Tessa said with both concern and awe in her voice. I started to formulate an explanation—something about how even after we leave the world, we are still a part of it. No, she would never understand that.

"That's cool, Daddy!" Tessa said before I could get a word out. She reached down with her little fingers and touched a wing that had come alive, and felt it tremble in the wind. I did the same.

"She can't fly, can she?" Tessa asked.

"No, not anymore," I said, now deciding to just answer the questions she asked. Then the wind died, the gull's wings fell back to her body, Tessa lost interest, and we continued down the beach.

✺

We should have buried Rosie right away, but the next three days after her death were just too busy with school activities. And Carol was often over at Ellen and John's. Neither of us was in the right frame of mind for a cat funeral, nor had the time to dig a grave. So I put Rosie in a two-gallon zip-lock plastic bag and cleared a little space for her in the freezer. The kids were not alarmed by a dead body in the freezer, since we did the same thing with Chip and Patch. Except in the hamsters' case, we kept them in there all winter because the ground had already frozen. As a joke to Carol, I wrote, "Oct. 2008: For Hamster Stew" on the bag label. She thought it was funny; Abby said I was "totally gross."

Saturday morning: I get up early to dig a grave in the backyard, but first pull Rosie out to let her thaw some. Her funeral is tonight. Bennett somehow senses what I am doing and soon appears in the backyard in his pajamas to watch me dig.

"Chip and Patch are right over there," he says.

"Yeah," I reply, "I'll bet they're both decayed by now." Bennett nods: "It's kind of like the stuff in the compost bin, isn't it?" he says. And I am pleased that he gets it, that he knows that bacteria and insects break the bodies of animals down just like they do melon rinds and orange peels. "Yep. Chip and Patch will turn into some really good soil," I say.

That evening, just after dusk, we all gather at Rosie's gravesite. I lay her mostly thawed body in the hole, and we all shovel some dirt in and say something we remember about her. Then I tamp the dirt down hard to prevent a coyote or a raccoon from trying to dig her up. Tessa puts a rock about the size of her hand on top of the grave, and Carol sets a small white candle on top of the rock. After she lights it, we stand quietly for a minute watching the tiny flame flicker against the growing darkness. Later that night, while the kids are getting ready for bed, I find them all gathered in the bathroom peering out the one window that looks out on the back yard.

"Look, Daddy," Abby says. "Rosie's candle is still burning."

The next day, while I'm mowing the backyard, Carol comes out waving and crying. "Ellen died," she says. "John just called." He has asked Carol to coordinate and lead the memorial service, which will be in a week. Ellen will be cremated.

The next day is crazy. Carol's dad calls: while bicycling at an Elderhostel in France, Carol's mom had become short of breath. They took her to a hospital in Paris to find blood clots in her lungs. The treatment was uncertain. It's frightening. And Tessa has just contracted a virulent flu. She has not been able to keep anything down for three days and is so dehydrated that we had to take her to the hospital. When they hooked her up to the IV, it was like her body woke from hibernation. "Oh, I feel better," she kept saying. When we arrive home from the hospital, I check the e-mail and find that my niece Sarah's son was just born—Stefan, a beautiful baby boy! He is nineteen and a half inches long, weighs eight pounds, one ounce, and is "nursing like a champ." The wonder and elation of the e-mail, of a new beginning, is welcome news amid all the death and illness.

Thinking of Sarah and Stefan, I sink back in my chair at the computer and close my eyes for a minute. I tune out AOL and Google and the frenetic circus of useless information at my fingertips, and fall back into memory—back into the timeless miracle of our children's births. Now, today, it seems that their lives have never stopped beginning, that the present and future have started to blur. Yet I remember those moments well: how the hours and minutes fell away so all that mattered was the soft, beautiful clock of Carol's body, and of Tessa's, and Abby's, and Bennett's. I remember the warm ticking of their blood, and each birth itself: the emergence of a wet and squirming animal, of a child, into the world. I remember their first cries, and their first sputtering breaths of oxygen, and how that breath soon fell into a rhythm, which has never stopped. It is a sacred rhythm—the fragile steady pulse of Creation—that they still carry, that we all do.

Chapter 14

Coyotes at the Mall

Predators and Prey

It is remarkable how many creatures live wild and free though secret in the woods, and still sustain themselves in the neighborhood of towns, suspected by hunters only.

HENRY DAVID THOREAU, *Walden*[1]

Two weeks after Ellen's death, I drive up to the cabin for a day and arrive late. It's cold, so I make a fire, pull a chair up to the stove, and take out a book. I'm reading an account of Thoreau's last days before his death from tuberculosis. When friends and family arrived in Concord in the spring of 1862 to pay their last respects, Thoreau was weak, but his mind was sharp. When his aunt asked him if he had made peace with God, he replied, "I didn't know that we had ever quarreled." One visitor, the Reverend Parker Pillsbury, couldn't resist a philosophical inquiry: "You seem so near the brink of a dark river," he said, "that I almost wonder how the opposite shore may appear to you." Thoreau's answer: "One world at a time."[2] In dying, he had given his old friend a five-word recipe for how to live. And now I have it as well. But tonight I'm too tired to consider all its implications. So I put the book away, push another log into the glowing stove, and crawl into my sleeping bag.

When I wake at dawn the next morning, the fire is out. Hoping to warm up, I pull on some clothes and go for a walk. A few minutes later, when I step out of the woods into a meadow, the first rays of the sun spill over the distant trees and bathe the field in a honey-colored light, turning it into the top of some holy mountain. I dig out my little notebook to record the image when, fifty feet ahead of me, a coyote springs out of the waist-high weeds like a furry jack-in-the-box and then pounces back down on something. When my heart recovers, I sneak a few steps closer to get a better look. He is bigger than I expect—maybe thirty-five pounds—his fur already thickening for winter. Crunching a mouse, he turns, sees me, and takes off. I'm close enough to hear a snorting breath when he bolts. I sprint after him like an idiot, crashing through the frosted weeds. I'm not sure why. I could never catch him, and if I did, what would I do? Yet my instinct is to follow, to get closer.

Ten seconds later he reappears two hundred yards ahead of me in the vineyard that abuts our land. He pauses, looks back at me as if amused, and disappears into the dried vines. This is only the third coyote I've seen here in five years. I hear them at night sometimes, and once found the remains of a deer kill that suggested coyotes. But I never see them. The coyotes always seem to be just out of sight—gray and brown ghosts loping in the mist along the edges of the day.

I grew up in Iowa—fishing and hunting and walking the woods and fields of my friends' farms—but I saw a coyote only once. And it was from a distance, at dusk, while baling hay. The first coyote I ever saw up close was in the suburbs, in Glen Ellyn. One morning, while I was jogging, the crash of a garbage can lid drew my eyes to a neighbor's driveway, where a thin, mangy dog was chewing on a wedge of pizza crust. He ran when he saw me. I later figured out it wasn't a dog, that coyotes and their families were moving to the burbs—and it wasn't for the schools. Since then, I have often seen coyotes in our neighborhood—walking through our backyard, and sleeping in the sun near the playground at Bennett's school.

Suburban coyotes do better than their country cousins. There's more to eat and good places to hide. Rural coyotes have a 30 percent chance of making it through their first year; urban coyotes are twice as likely to survive that long.[3] In rural areas, the leading cause of coyote death is hunting or trapping; for urban coyotes, it's cars. So suburban towns with slow traffic speeds and large parks or forest preserves—places like Glen Ellyn—are a more likely place to see coyotes than here in the woods.

Last year, a teacher in suburban Chicago was walking through a large mall parking lot back to her minivan when she noticed a thin animal slinking between the rows of cars and slowly coming toward her. Suddenly, the coyote lunged for her miniature poodle, clamping his jaws around the dog's hindquarters. She grabbed the head and for thirty seconds, there, in the parking lot, the sixty-year-old high school teacher and the coyote had a tug-of-war. It ended when she managed to pick up and throw a shopping bag full of clothes at the coyote, which finally let go and ran off.

Lured by the smell of sizzling meat, a coyote recently strolled through the propped open door of a Quiznos on Adams Street in downtown Chicago. The owner at first thought it was a dog. The docile thirty-pound canine walked past the counter without ordering and lay down on a stack of Diet Pepsi in an open cooler and stayed there. Though he remained quiet, two of the four patrons left immediately; the other two stayed and finished their chicken sandwiches. A large crowd of passersby and tourists soon gathered at the front window to see the wild visitor and snap pictures. An hour later an animal-control officer arrived with a catchpole and worked the thrashing animal back to his van.

No one knows where that coyote came from. They catch ten or fifteen in the city center every year, but usually closer to a likely home: a lakefront park, an isolated trash dump, or a patch of trees near the railroad tracks. This coyote would have had to weave through a half mile of bumper-to-bumper traffic and harried shoppers and soapbox preachers to reach the Quiznos.

Having given up on the coyote I surprised in the meadow, I walk back toward our cabin. The sun is burning the frost off. Some cottonwood leaves, which have already turned from yellow to brown, swirl in the breeze. The oaks are still pink and orange, but they, too, are turning toward winter. A deer hears me and breaks for safety, his white tail flashing as he bounds over the brush and disappears deeper into the woods. Unlike coyotes, deer are common here. Because lone coyotes hunt deer fawns, and coyote packs sometimes will hunt adults, it seems the deer alone might draw more coyotes to this land.

I sit down in the cabin to read a stack of news articles about coyotes. My favorite is about O'Hare Airport: two jets temporarily aborted their landings because a pack of coyotes was hunting on their landing strip. And airport workers often see them trotting along the runways. In the last fifteen years, twenty-three coyotes have been hit by airplanes in Illinois. Cars I understand, but airplanes? Though I suppose "runway kill" is a sign not just of the explosion of coyotes in Chicago, but of the wild escalation in the number of planes and flights in the last twenty years. About eighty million people passed through O'Hare last year. There are 2,500 flights per day. It's not just the coyotes who are on the move.

All these odd intersections of coyote and human lives point to the shrinking habitat we share. And though most of the 2,000 or so coyotes that live in Chicago remain unseen, the number of encounters with people is increasing.

These chance confrontations with urban coyotes excite us. Because they don't belong there. Because they somehow wandered into our high-tech, climate-controlled world. Because a coyote sparks a deep nostalgia for the wild, for the natural world we've conquered and nearly destroyed. They spark the memory of ourselves as animals.

But urban coyotes also frighten us. Because they don't belong there. Because no one wants their miniature dachshund eaten as a midnight snack, or to be sitting in a lawn chair some evening in a carefully pruned yard and turn to see a dirty, shifty animal stealing a pork chop off a stainless-steel gas grill. The coyote reminds us: we may be animals, but we are not *wild* animals. If you want wild, try the Nature Channel.

Yet beyond the excitement and fear the coyote provokes, and beyond the wildness it represents, is the simple truth that for good or ill, our lives are tangled together.

The coyote's arrival into our territory is less an intrusion than a natural migration—from the once plentiful fields and woodlands to the islands of available habitat that dot Chicago's westward sprawl. By necessity, they are moving from the disappearing "country" to the suburbs, and the city. And this movement is aided by the network of forest preserves and parks and the green corridors that connect them. Like sparrows and dandelions and people, coyotes adapt well to changing and disturbed environments. They flourish on the edges of biocommunities, which are divided and multiplied by each new road or subdivision or golf course or shopping mall we build. It's getting edgier all the time.

The coyote's booming success in the suburbs is tied to the success of another edge species: the Canada goose. The beautiful honking Vs crossing the sky in October, heading south, were also once a lovely emblem of the "wild" in the Midwest. But their population exploded in the 1980s and '90s.[4] Now, many don't fly south but rather live in the suburbs year-round, on huge, well-mowed corporate-center lawns near warm retention ponds.

Several hundred Canada geese live on the grounds around the building where I teach. I arrived there one afternoon several years ago to see a goose looking out at me like an anxious student from behind a glass door. Someone had let (or lured) him into the small glass foyer between the entrance doors (which lead to the carpeted classrooms) and the exit doors (which lead back outside). Totally confused by the whirring fluorescent lights and the transparent walls on both sides, he went crazy when I opened the door. Hissing and snapping, he tried to fly through the exterior glass doors to the grass and sky on the other side. *Whump!* The collision stunned him. I opened the door, and he stumbled out.

As with the coyotes, such stories are common. And though I felt sorry for that bewildered goose, many people have lost their sympathy. Due to their aggression at nesting time, and the environmental degradation caused by their feces, geese can be a nuisance. This attitude is confirmed by the new "Geese Police" companies, which specialize in goose removal, and by the growing arsenal of goose-eradication products you can find at the local hardware store.

Given the growing intolerance with the Chicago geese invasion of the 1990s, it was not surprising that a landmark study of the goose population in 2000 drew a lot of attention. It showed that the once soaring population had abruptly halted.

What happened? Canada geese, with their size and strength, can often fight off raccoons and foxes and mink and prevent them from eating their eggs and goslings. But they are no match for a coyote. A single animal or a small band of coyotes can pillage an entire nesting ground in one or two evenings, stealing dozens of eggs and caching those they don't eat right away for a later meal.[5] In a few years, the coyotes cut the annual growth rate of the Canada goose population in Chicagoland from nearly 20 percent to less than 2 percent.

Urban coyotes have curbed Chicago's goose population and kept the deer and rodent population in check, and they don't attack people. Yet they are still considered outsiders, dangerous, not welcome. The fear and worry they conjure seems to outweigh our nostalgia over their wildness. As I sit in the cabin tonight, I wonder why that is, why we think the coyotes belong someplace else—someplace like here, in this yet undeveloped land, rather than in Glen Ellyn. And I wonder why it seems so bizarre to see five coyotes in the burbs for each one I see here in the woods. The same is true for skunks and red foxes. I'm not sure who belongs where anymore. But maybe that's the point. As the boundaries between country, suburb, and city, and between forest, farm, and factory, have blurred, so has the idea of the "wild."

Last week I saw an ad for an Amtrak train line from downtown Chicago to New Buffalo. The commute takes just ninety minutes from Chicago and is expected to catalyze more new housing developments—not just more summer homes for the tourist town, but subdivisions for permanent residents who will work in the city. It is certainly better to train to work than to drive, and for people to belong to a community rather than just vacation there, but I had never thought that Chicago would stretch north around the lake this far. Or that this little cabin we cobbled together here in the woods might someday be part of a Chicago suburb. But I think it's possible, which is ironic, and depressing, and a bit amusing. Particularly now, as I walk through the woods, watching and wondering when the new neighbors will arrive, when the coyotes will move in.

Chapter 15

The Art of Dying
Art and Activism

What is the price-current of an honest man and patriot to-day?
They hesitate, and they regret, and sometimes they petition;
but they do nothing in earnest and with effect. They will wait,
well disposed, for others to remedy the evil, that they may no
longer have it to regret.

HENRY DAVID THOREAU[1]

I had planned on going to the cabin today. But I have too many
papers to grade, a book review that is past due, and a list of projects
around the house to finish. So I work through a stack of papers,
finish the review, send it off, and then start in on the mountain
range of dirty clothes in our basement. After washing and folding
a few loads of clothes, I reglue a kitchen chair that has fallen apart
and take the compost out to the bin. But by late morning I start
to feel uneasy, and I'm not sure why. And then, at the top of the
hour, the BBC news cycle repeats its headline story, and I figure
out what's bugging me. I'd been listening to radio reports all morning about a bombing in Iraq that killed a dozen civilians. And
that's not all that's bothering me. All morning I've also been walk-

ing past the flyer Carol posted on the fridge about the American Friends Service Committee's Die-In at Chicago's Federal Plaza. It's today—in about two hours. Dan had told me about it too, but I had e-mailed that I couldn't attend. All of a sudden, though, something in me wants to go, knows I should go. I check my watch; there is still time. I could be back before the kids get out of school and Carol gets home from work.

Then I think of Tessa. Maybe I could zip by the high school and bring her along, too. It would be a good experience. We've dragged her and Abby and Bennett along to plenty of demonstrations before, and they always rise to the occasion. But no, it wouldn't be fair without first talking to her. Too last minute. She's got a lot going on at school. I'll do this one alone.

I call the number on the flyer and ask whether it's too late for me to join the demonstration. "No, it's fine," the woman says. "Please come, but bring your own sheet." She gives me an address where we are to meet in a little over an hour for a brief orientation. From there we will silently walk a few blocks to the Federal Plaza.

༚

Before I know it, I'm lying on my back on concrete in the heart of Chicago while chaos whirs around me. After my harried stop-and-go drive into the Loop, I'm a bit worked up, so I try to calm down, to get centered, and to let the warm light streaming down through the geometry of steel and glass become what it is—a prayer of forgiveness. But this only partly works. We need *a lot* of forgiveness these days. And I'm distracted—by the abrupt carbonic hiss of a bus pulling out into traffic and the sudden *rat-a-tat-tat* of a jackhammer breaking up a sidewalk somewhere. It sounds close.

My feet are a few inches away from the feet of the *Flamingo*, a four-story-high Calder sculpture in the middle of the plaza. It has always looked like a big chicken to me, as if it should be titled *Big Red Chicken Stalks Inner City*. Because I have covered myself with a white sheet and am pretending to be dead, I can't see the red chicken. But I imagine it looming over me, coming to life, pecking at my soft flesh and at the other bodies lying around me. Given the tenor of the moment—pretending to be dead and all— I should be more serious, but the chicken keeps scratching around in my brain.

I dream of the FBI director making an emergency announcement that the Calder Chicken and the equally worrisome Picasso sculpture in Daley Plaza are terrorist robots electronically connected to a Henri Moore sculpture in the Chicago Art Institute. Reportedly planted long ago by a sleeper cell of starving artists, they can be simultaneously activated at any moment. "We are all vulnerable to such attacks," they might say. "The enemy is everywhere. Even in modern art."

But here's the thing: this daydream is no more absurd than war itself—or than I am, lying here wrapped in a sheet in the middle of a huge city on a busy workday, just a few feet from the honking congestion of Dearborn and Adams streets. The die-in is an art installation. The organizers are artists. I am a piece of art. Our forty bodies and forty white sheets and forty red carnations have been arranged on the cement canvas into a death grid, a graveyard. We symbolize the number of Iraqis who die every day from the war. We seek to create the antithesis of war—art—and through it a reverence for life.

Yet not everyone sees it that way. I lie in the darkness and wonder how many passersby are baffled by our method and motives. The pretty young woman who walked up to me as we approached the plaza and stuck her right middle finger in my face, and smiled angrily, might say that we do it because we want attention, because we want to be seen. She is right, in part. But I think it is more about learning how to see, about finding ourselves in the eyes of "the enemy," about understanding the fragile yet essential weave of our distant lives.

The point of our connection is not "freedom" or "democracy"

or some vague ideology. We share a shrinking, polluted planet, and a perilous dependence on oil. We share the need for food and sleep and clean water. We share the fear of death, and the agony of sending our loved ones to fight and die. We share the need to love and be loved. We share the longing for beauty, and the truth of art against the lie of war—forty live bodies lying dead in the middle of the Federal Plaza.

Several years ago, U.S. military leaders watched the destruction of the Iraqi national museum and library, but the soldiers on the ground were ordered not to *see* it—not to see the looting of history, the theft of memory, the bashing of ancient vases and paintings, the burning of sacred texts, the crushing of the cradle of *someone else's* civilization. But it is also ours, connected by a cross-cultural bridge that was never built, or imagined—between religion and art, Islam and Christianity, Iraqis and Americans. We *are* related—in many concrete ways. The biblical patriarch Abraham was also a Muslim prophet who hailed from the Iraqi city of Ur. Nineveh, where Jonah (also a Christian *and* a Muslim prophet) was said to have preached after being swallowed by a whale and miraculously disgorged, is part of modern-day Mosul. And the putative site of the mythic Garden of Eden is located in southern Iraq.

I'm not sure how U.S. history got so disconnected from the rest of the world's, nor why it keeps getting shorter, why it must always be new and improved. It began a couple of centuries ago with a bunch of angry colonists fighting for their freedom, which is supposedly what we are defending in Iraq and Afghanistan, which is why I'm lying here. Which points to the problem: our best and only defense seems to be an offense—the art of war—whose goal is to destroy rather than to create.

On September 12, 2001—after the skies were emptied of planes and we were assured the Sears Tower would not be hit—I had an urge to visit the Chicago Art Institute, to counter the tragedy in New York with O'Keeffe's voluptuous lilies, Hopper's gritty streetscapes, Pollock's wild spatters. But parts of the city were closed down, and so were some parts of me—lost in the spiral of sadness—so I settled for a coffee table book of Chagall's paintings. As I leafed through the stunning images, while the grainy towers fell over and over on TV, I wondered how Chagall would have depicted the absurdity of the planes turned missiles, of the people leaping into the flaming concrete canyon. What would he have seen, and created, in the face of the destroyed?

I have been dead for only a few minutes when someone drops a long-stemmed carnation on my chest. It lands on top of my folded hands. The soft, sudden weight of the flower is an epiphany, a moment of attention that connects me, reminds me that I belong to everything and everyone, that we are all related. I feel it deeply—the flower, the sun, the wind, their quiet resilience and forgiveness.

A gull screams. I imagine the feathered, flattened M coasting high above me, glowing in the sunlight, then veering to the east—a white silhouette pumping through a four-block corridor of skyscraping shadows that finally opens on to the lake and sky—a watercolor painting that has no borders, no endings. Today it would be all shades of blue, broken only by a few intermittent clouds and whitecaps. From under the white sheet, I imagine the lake at a great distance: a shimmering blue body whose fingers touch other lakes, whose branches feed into rivers, which empty into oceans, which reach around the world and touch the soil, the homes, the daily lives, of every enemy we have ever appointed or imprisoned or shot or carpet-bombed in the name of freedom or of God. Whether we call them collateral damage or terrorists or people, we are closely related. Closer all the time.

A woman with a cheap microphone and little beat-up amplifier begins to sing the names of the dead. She nurses vibrant and haunting tones out of the cracking, echo-y sound system: "Rafid Naji Hasan, nine years old; Jumma Ibrahim, fourteen years old; Fadhel Mohammed al Dulaimi, forty-five years old . . ." The names go on and on.

I lie in the darkness and replay in my mind the BBC radio

story I heard this morning: "Today the U.S. military attacked a large compound in Sadr City where there were suspected insurgents. Forty-one al-Qaeda terrorists were killed." An hour later the Iraqi government announced that sixteen of the dead were confirmed civilians, including a nine-month-old, a three-year-old, and a seven-year-old, who was literally blown into pieces. I try to imagine the weeping father of the seven-year-old collecting his son's severed arm and leg in a cardboard box.

What is an average citizen on the other side of the ocean to do with such terror? How are we to respond to this "democratic" slaughter, this terrifying "freedom"? What *do* you do? Lie down on the cement in the middle of the city in the middle of the day and pretend you're dead?

I have been teaching Thoreau's "Civil Disobedience" in my freshman composition classes. In it, Thoreau critiques the U.S. government and military and all those who serve the state with their bodies and heads, but not their conscience: "I think that it is not too soon for honest men to rebel and revolutionize. What makes this duty the more urgent is the fact that the country so overrun is not our own, but ours is the invading army."

I don't expect my students to take to the streets when they read this, enraged at Thoreau's startling relevance. Some could not care less. Some are offended by his "anti-American" sentiment. But a few are angry and frustrated. And even though they are overwhelmed—with full-time school, full-time jobs, and families—they wonder what they can do. They approach me after class. I tell them I am bewildered too. Here we are, watching Vietnam all over again. How can this be happening? "It's weird," says Frank, a student and soldier who just returned from Iraq. "We are afraid to lose, or to surrender, yet we can't clearly define what 'winning' is."

Soon the class will read sections from *Walden* and learn that Thoreau's politics stem less from ideology than from a deep reverence for life rooted in his love of the natural world. He knew the politics of the pine tree and the loon as well as those of the

Mexican-American War. So though he sometimes briefly kept run-away slaves in his cabin at the pond, it was perhaps less due to abolitionist politics than to his knowing that the slaves' quest for freedom was also his own, that they belonged equally to Creation.

I have been dead for a long time when I finally catch the sweet, delicate scent of my carnation—just a trace, and only for a second. A pigeon coos as he struts along the edge of my sheet, snagging his little claw in the fabric but managing to shake it free. Then a little girl—one of the children of the temporarily dead—starts giggling about something. Her clicking shoes skip through the odd labyrinth of flower-adorned bodies.

I think of my own kids and begin to wonder about the time. But I can't lift my arm to read my watch without disturbing the art. I need to leave right at two o'clock to make it to Lincoln Elementary by the first bell to meet Bennett. Abby has to be taken to soccer, and Tessa needs a lift home from a cross-country meet. What the hell: I slowly turn my arm and raise it so I can see that I have been lying here for twenty minutes. It seems like an hour.

I'm not even sure why I came to this demonstration. I need to go grocery shopping, and I have stacks of papers to grade. Was it guilt? Yes, partly. The belief that I'm making a difference? Maybe. The hope that this theater of the absurd will help alleviate the suffering of the Iraqi people? Perhaps. I'm not really sure. My motivations seem less noble, less clear. I'm just trying to learn how to believe in something, how to see in the dark.

"... Ahmad Mahdey Jaleel, twenty-three years old; Tahad Saeed Abas, nine months old; Thea Mhed Kder, eleven years old; Zina Ali Hirat, three years old; Abra Kata Albdwe, seventy years old ..."

It is Thea, the eleven-year-old girl, whose name I cannot let go. My daughters are eleven and fourteen. Thea. I see her skipping rope in the red clay dust behind her home in Najaf, perhaps munching on a sour green mango with a friend. Thea. I see her exasperated face when her parents say her bombed-out school will not be reopened. Thea. I see her lithe body running wildly away from something. What is it? What is she running from? Thea. I see the name wheeling up toward the sun like a dove that has been released so it can return home. Thea. The enemy. A dead little girl. Her. Me. Us.

My mind wanders to a recent phone call. One of my students called at 7:00 a.m. to tell me he would miss class because his cousin was killed the previous day in Iraq. I found a notice about the death and a picture of his cousin in the local paper the next day: he was twenty-four years old. According to the paper, he "died from wounds suffered in an attack in Anbar province, a hotbed of the Sunni insurgency." It was his second tour of duty. He had "three great loves in his life: his family, the outdoors, and the Marines."

At some point I completely zone out and just ride the river of Iraqi names, the singing of the dead. And that's when it happens. A strong wind comes out of nowhere and pulls out the corners of my sheet, which begin to flap like little flags. Then, suddenly, the carnation is gone—abruptly lifted from my chest by a gust of wind.

How odd it is to imagine the flight of the flower into the sky rather than to see it. I want to pull back the sheet to confirm I am right. I want clarity, the comfort of a fact. I want to *know*. Instead, I fall back into the river of names. I lie in the darkness and drift with the dead. I see the clean-cut face of my student's cousin, and a few thousand other dead Americans. Their bodies and faces float by in my nightmare. But it is the eyes that haunt me. They never close, but are fixed in disbelief.

". . . Abaas Haloob Mataar, nineteen years old; Karar Harmeed Abed Ali, two years old; Abas Hamza, eighty years old; Abas Zire Agel, five years old; Iman Zowaer Ohlaa, seven years old; Wahaab Halmaan Monsor, twenty-eight years old . . ."

When the singing of names stops, a new voice echoes over the scratchy PA. He cites a new British study that reports that 1.2 million Iraqis, half of whom are civilians, have died in the war. He says the die-in is a reminder of the reality of war for those who cannot imagine that scale of suffering.

I imagine a literal scale, with the U.S. Congress and the president lifted high above the gruesome wars they wage. In a shining gold hors d'oeuvres tray, they sit in leather chairs, bloated with food, oblivious to the immense weight, the huge heap of bodies in the rusted barrel on the other side of the fulcrum. I like this metaphor, until I start to wonder if I would have to place myself in the golden tray too. Where else is there? The only answer I can think of is *here*, now, waiting in the darkness, trying to learn the art of dying.

The woman starts to sing the names again. Then someone gently lays the carnation back on my chest, on my folded hands. The startling weight and scent of the flower again pulls me toward the heart of things, reminds me why we're here, and what the artist knows: that all life is deeply and intimately connected. That we are all created and forgiven by the sun and wind and water. That in the shiny-wet eyes of the enemy is the clear reflection of ourselves. And that victory can begin with a lonely act of surrender.

Chapter 16

Cougars in the Corn

Facts and Truths

"I, too, would fain set down something beside facts.
Facts should only be as the frame to my pictures; they
should be material to the mythology I am writing. . . ."

HENRY DAVID THOREAU, *Journal*[1]

When I came across these lines in Thoreau's *Journal* today, I
thought of the papers my freshman composition students wrote
last week. I brought the papers with me to the cabin because I have
to return them on Monday and they take a long time to grade.
I like the assignment: the students read three very different articles
about the event that occurred on December 30, 1890, at Wounded
Knee Creek in South Dakota. One version is from the local newspaper editor, who was at the battle site the day after. Another is
from the letters of a cavalry sergeant who was in the battle. And
another is from a Lakota medicine man, who was nine at the time,
and arrived in the middle of the fighting.[2] Usually, *none* of my
students have even heard of the event, so they don't know who to
believe: the writer who says it was an "engagement," the one who
calls it a "battle," or the one who calls it a "massacre." One version
blames the savage Indians. Another blames the cavalry. One claims

the 250 Indians killed themselves in the mayhem of the cross-fire. Another claims the cavalry planned the massacre the night before. The assignment: read all three versions of the event, compare and contrast the "facts" and "evidence," and—without using the Internet or any other sources—decide which one is *true*.

In every class, at least some students choose each of the three versions of the event as the "truth." Which is the point of the assignment: truth is relative—an interpreted reality—as is "fact," when used to construct a truth.

I start in on the papers. One student argues that the sergeant's version is the most factual because it includes a lot of numbers. Another believes the sergeant because "he saw it with his own eyes." Two other students make the same claim for the Lakota writer. Then I find the same line in a paper arguing for the newspaper editor. As I read through the papers, no matter which version they choose, this claim often comes up: "He saw it with his own eyes." But only a few students ever mention that how and why and when the writer "saw" determines what "it" is.

After grading one class's papers, my focus starts to wane. So I crack a beer and turn to some lighter reading: the local paper. I picked one up at the Sawyer grocery today because of the headline: "Cougar Sighting in Berrien County." But when I read on, I find that the evidence of the cougar's presence is not a tuft of hair or scat or tracks, but a blurry digital photo taken with a cell phone. When I first looked at the picture, I couldn't tell where the cougar was. No matter how I squinted, I just couldn't see it. Then I decided it was probably the small, dark shape on the edge of the cornfield. But it also kind of looked like a black Lab or a coyote or a bobcat, or maybe the Loch Ness Monster. There have been thousands of such "sightings" of wild cougars recorded in the Midwest throughout the last decade. Though some of these accounts are true and some likely aren't, each one stokes a remarkable story—that wild mountain lions have returned to the Midwest and formed a small but viable population after more than a century of absence.

It was on a cool, fall morning when I first heard about the wild cougars in southwest Michigan. I rode my bike into Sawyer that day and was puzzled by a dozen or so life-size plywood cutouts of some animal—a tiger or some big catlike thing with a long tail. I had no idea what the animal was or what the point was. They were all spray-painted black like silhouettes and set up in front of the post office, the grocery, and the drugstore—as if the whole town had become an amusement park overnight. I went into the post office and asked about them.

"You don't know about the cougars?" The postmistress smiled. "They keep seeing them. One attacked a horse last week."

"I heard about someone seeing one cougar, but not cougars," I said. "And I thought it was an escaped pet."

"Well, they're not sure, but it sounds like there could be several. They've seen the tracks too."

"Do they have any scat or DNA confirmation?"

"Not yet, but I think it's coming."

Just as I was leaving, an older woman who had been listening inside earlier waved at me from her car. I walked over and she rolled down her window. "Just so you know that it's true," she said, "I saw one along Warren Woods Road last month—early morning, on the way to town—big and sleek, with a long tail. And when it ran, it leaped over the ditch onto the road just like a lion. I mean, we don't have animals like that around here. It wasn't a bobcat or a coyote or a deer. What else could it be? I called the DNR [Department of Natural Resources], and they took down the info, but I know they didn't believe me. No one's going to believe it until someone shoots one—which is kind of sad."

She rolled her window back up and looked satisfied and relieved, as if she had done her duty. I looked up the story about the horse, and sure enough, there were pictures in the local paper of a large thoroughbred that had been mauled to death. After a three-hour autopsy, a local vet and the Michigan Wildlife Conservancy called the event "a confirmed cougar attack." The most "factual" evidence: the size and pattern of the claw marks themselves. The Michigan DNR, however, based on its own review of the case, determined that the horse had been attacked by coyotes or dogs.

A few weeks later, jogging on the beach of nearby Warren Dunes State Park, I ran into a middle-aged local man, James, who claimed he had seen black panthers several times there in the park. "Oh, they're here. That's a fact. They're just secretive—hard to see," he said. "Sometimes they come down to the water in the early morning to drink—or to track deer that are going down to drink." An avid walker who often roams the woods along the lake, James added that his most recent cougar sighting was a year prior—a black panther and its single offspring. "You should really keep a pistol with you if you go back in the woods around here," he warned. I didn't ask him if he carried one, but I asked why the park officials didn't post warning signs if it was dangerous. "Oh, they're covering it up," James said. "They're worried it will harm tourism. I can't confirm it, but I've heard from several people that the DNR is shooting them from helicopters in the winter to keep the population down—to prevent any hysteria from tourists."

James seemed like an honest person, but I had no idea what to do with his stories. So I went to the park rangers and asked them. They had never seen any cougars in the park or anywhere else in Michigan and said they weren't a threat. They chuckled at my inquiry about cougars being culled from helicopters. "We have more problems with raccoons," one ranger said.

I don't know who to believe. There have been over a thousand reported cougar sightings in Michigan in the three years since I first encountered those plywood silhouettes in Sawyer. Last year alone there were 383. So today, as I walk from the cabin back toward the river, I'm starting to wonder how they all could be wrong. Even if one in ten were accurate, that was still a lot of cougars—enough that one would likely drift across our land from time to time.

The more I think about it, the more curious I become. And uneasy. I find a stout oak branch and break it off so it has a sharp end. I never use walking sticks, but today it seems like a good idea. Then something rustles in the distance—maybe a coyote, but more likely a deer. We have a lot of deer—which many claim is what has drawn the cougars out of the Dakotas and further east in the first place.

This gets me thinking about those three partially eaten deer carcasses Dan found last year in the woods. No one was sure what had killed and eaten them. It could have been coyotes, but they usually take fawns rather than adults.

When I reach the banks of the Galien, I remember something else: mountain lions like to follow river corridors when hunting. Great. Now there's only one thing on my mind: where is it hiding? Perhaps in one of those hollow beech logs?

Like a kid checking his closet for monsters before going to bed at night, I walk over with my oak stick and inspect each of the rotten trees. Nope. Both are empty. Feeling a little silly, I instinctively look around to be sure no one else is out walking, that no one has seen me check the trees. How ridiculous. An Ohio biologist writes that the chances of seeing a wild cougar in the Midwest are much lower than being hit by space debris.

In spite of my embarrassing-but-real apprehension, I keep following the river deeper into the woods, back toward the herons' nests. And that's when it happens: five huge whitetail deer tear out of the river bottom in a frantic sprint and scare the shit out of me. Were they flushed out by a cougar? Then, a few seconds later, a wild turkey perched in an unseen oak branch a few feet away from my head suddenly detonates, blasting into the wet air with a crazed squawk. I whirl in fear and instinctively try to recall the prescribed response to a cougar in the woods (which I had memorized from a DNR pamphlet): 1) Face the animal and do not act submissive. Stand tall, wave your arms, and talk in a loud voice. 2) Never run. If children are present, pick them up so they cannot run. 3) If attacked, fight back with whatever is available. DO NOT play dead.

And then, ten seconds later, the deer have gone back to their foraging, and the turkey to some other tree, and I recognize what has just happened. Nothing. *Nothing.* I walk deeper into the woods and try to figure out why I'm so edgy. Maybe it's simply that I've never seen a cougar in the wild—and only once in a zoo. Which prompts me to rely too heavily on my imagination, on the places where I *have* seen wild cougars: on television and in movies, on *Gunsmoke* and *Bonanza* and in various "westerns."

I remember one scene where a huge cougar roared from atop a mound of rock, startling a cowboy on the trail below him. The hero whirled to face his own death while also somehow aiming his rifle in the general direction of the now airborne cougar, hoping to kill it on the way down. Then the gunshot, and the large, furry body landing on the cowboy, partially concealing him for just a second. So you weren't quite sure whether he had killed it, or whether it would spring up and rip him to shreds. But the cougar was of course dead, and the hero crawled out from under the carcass, brushed himself off, and said something like, "That was close."

Yet those movies were not called *mid*westerns. They weren't supposed to take place in Illinois or Michigan or Iowa. Cougars are not called *field* lions. Here, there are no mountains, nor the vast tracks of wilderness cougars require. So what are they doing haunting the cornfields and vineyards of southwest Michigan?

No one is sure. In the nineteenth century wild cougars flourished throughout the United States. But increased settlement, hunting, the fur trade, and dwindling deer numbers all pushed them west. Now, however, they are an endangered species, and this protection, along with the booming deer population in the Midwest, could be luring them back. Most wildlife biologists believe that the nearest breeding cougar colony is in South Dakota (with around 200 animals). But some think that there's already a small colony here, in the Midwest—that like the coyotes, cougars are learning to adapt and survive amid the small remnants of wilderness that remain.

The Michigan Wildlife Conservancy is convinced that cougars have recolonized in Michigan's Upper Peninsula, which does have a significant tract of wilderness. The MWC has been conducting field research for a decade and has discovered dozens of "significant" bits of evidence: tracks, scat, and cougar- killed deer, as well as many convincing photos and videos (some of which include cougar kittens.) This and other verifiable research has even prompted the Michigan DNR—known by some as cougar deniers—to confirm that the rare mountain lion does wander into Michigan from time to time. But the DNR claims there is no real evidence of a breeding population.

It was about a month after my harrowing nonencounter with a mountain lion along the Galien River that a *real* wild cougar appeared in Winnetka, a Chicago suburb. A day later it showed up in Roscoe Village, on Chicago's North Side. Neighbor after stunned neighbor reported seeing a large mountain lion bounding through a network of residential backyards before leaping a six-foot privacy fence and finding itself confined in a side yard. There it was cornered by five Chicago police officers, who said they shot it because it had turned on them and they had no other options. The picture of the officers standing over the dead 150-pound mountain lion in the *Chicago Tribune* is bizarre, as if they have been on some weird urban safari and are posing with a trophy no one really wanted to take home. It was just a little too exotic, even stranger than a coyote in a Quiznos.

Shortly after the cougar was killed in Chicago, a number of other sightings were reported in Michigan and Illinois. One was in Wheaton, the little town next door to us here in Glen Ellyn. The eyewitness, who was jogging through a park, said she saw a huge, dark-colored cat slink into the weeds—a "black cougar" that was much larger than her sixty-pound dog.

A few days later, a biologist from a local zoo made impressions of the paw prints in the mud and quickly determined that it was not a cougar, but most likely a house cat. In his report, he noted that there have been only two other confirmed cougar encounters in Illinois in recent years: a cougar was hit by a train in southern Illinois in 2000, and, in 2004, a bow hunter shot one in western Illinois. Prior to that, the last known appearance of a cougar in the state was in 1864. The report also noted that there has never been a "black" cougar captured or recorded in the United States.

At about the same time as the Wheaton sighting, a large "black panther" was reported hiding in a cement drain pipe in a park outside Warren, a little town near Detroit. I listened to the anonymous 911 call: "I'm not playing games," the caller told the dispatcher. "I went up behind it and shined a light in there—and it's huge. It's like a 150-pound cat." Ten police officers then rushed to the scene to investigate, where they could see what looked like a large animal in the drain pipe looking out at them. After identifying the cougar, they retreated to a safe distance for fear it would lunge at them. The DNR advised them to tranquilize the animal, but it would take ten minutes for the drug to work, and that seemed dangerous. So, after almost an hour on the site conferring, they decided to tase the animal. A police sergeant carefully aimed, fired, and hit the animal, but there was no movement. So then the policeman, in an action calling to mind a modern-day Barney Fife, cautiously proceeded toward the wild animal and discovered that it was stuffed—a life-size toy cougar someone had carefully positioned in the drain.

That prankster knew how to muddy "the truth," and "the facts," and how to blur the tenuous line between the real and the imagined, between what you see and what you think you see. Which is probably why, in spite of all the confirmed sightings of mountain lions and all the proof that they are wandering back into the Midwest, the truth remains relative. There may be a small, reclusive breeding colony of mountain lions somewhere nearby. Or most of the sightings may be false, with the exception of a few random cougars who occasionally stray a long way from home. The problem is that human truth always involves human imagination. And what many call "the facts" are open to interpretation: the hundreds of footprints and photos and videos are all *relatively* factual. The DNA samples and the cougar carcasses are not. Such empirical evidence is irrefutable, but there is very little of it. So what does one do with all this evidence or nonevidence? How does one tell the whole story with integrity?

Since that day when I first rode into Sawyer and saw all those black cougars, I've figured out that the plywood silhouettes are also part of a good-hearted marketing scheme. During the summer tourist season, the cougar cutouts help pique interest in the town and get people talking. And they suggest that even southwest Michigan is wild—a pristine wilderness area you should visit. Though there are no bears or moose, as in the Upper Peninsula, perhaps there is a mountain lion or two. And this alluring myth of the wild is reinforced by the new state motto, which I read on a big sign whenever I cross the state line from Indiana: "Welcome to *Pure* Michigan."

This corner of Michigan, with its orchards and winding country roads and beaches, *is* lovely. But is it pure? During my lifetime, the lake, rivers, air, and soil have all been polluted by industry, agriculture, and new development. You can eat only certain fish, and only so many per month. Some days you can't swim in the lake, because the E. coli count is too high. So can it really be called "unspoiled nature," as the radio ads proclaim? And should we really believe that wild cougars hunt deer amid these scattered woodlots and sprawling fields?

After reviewing all the research and evidence and rumors I could find on the topic, I've finally decided that the answer is no. And yes. And maybe. It just all depends on where you're standing, and where you look, and for how long, and what you are able to see, and what you choose to ignore.

WINTER

But the winter was not given to us
for no purpose. We must thaw its cold
with our genialness. We are tasked to find out
and appropriate all the nutriment it yields.
If it is a cold and hard season, its fruit, no doubt,
is the more concentrated and nutty. . . .

HENRY DAVID THOREAU, *Journal*[1]

Chapter 17

A Familiar Darkness
Desperation and Deliberation

The light which puts out our eyes is darkness to us. Only that day dawns to which we are awake. There is more day to dawn. The sun is but a morning star.

HENRY DAVID THOREAU, *Walden*[1]

Chicago winters baffle me. The days alternate between gray, bitter, and freezing, and gray, muddy, and thawing. The kids layer on coats when it's cold but run around in T-shirts when it warms up. So they get sick. It's the season of eternal phlegm, of hissing vaporizers and silver teaspoons full of gooey, bubble-gum-flavored syrups that break fevers and dry up noses and end midnight coughs. All kinds of coughs: whooping coughs, barking coughs, wheezing coughs, hacking coughs, sniffling coughs. Some are wet, some dry; some are in the throat, some in the chest; some are from allergy, some from colds, and some from a mysterious planet called Virus. In the middle of the night, though, I'm not awake enough to classify coughs. I'm just trying to locate from which room they are coming.

Like last night: I again found myself wandering around in the darkness with Carol. We were both trying to figure out which kid was coughing and who needed what. Bennett was barking and needed more humidity and some VapoRub smeared on his chest. Abby was hacking and needed a decongestant and to be turned on her side. Tessa's sniffling and labored snore was a sinus infection. She needed antibiotics. Later, I fell asleep sitting up in a chair in the study holding a spoon and an open bottle of green menthol cough syrup. I awoke in the darkness, unsure where I was, but figured it out when I felt the syrup dripping on my leg. The bottle had tipped over, the green sap pooling in my lap before running down my leg onto the oak floor. After wiping up the sticky mess, I checked the digital clock on the desk: 4:05 a.m.

Unable to fall back asleep, I'm still sitting here in the study now—paging through Thoreau's *Journal* and trying to get sleepy. I scan the winter entries from the 1850s in search of some regret or sorrow to match my own. "January," he writes, "is the hardest month to get through."[2] He describes a time he "began to grow torpid when exposed a long time to the pinching winter air."[3] But these entries eventually turn hopeful. In the end, the winter passages are nearly as full of joy and wonder as the other months. It's depressing.

Mr. Positive even celebrates the beauty of gray skies, finds the icy cold invigorating, and blithely suggests that winter should inspire rather than tire us: "We all feel somewhat confined by the winter; the nights are longer and we sleep more. Yet the thought is not less active; perhaps it is more so."[4]

"Somewhat" confined? Doesn't he have days when the intellect shuts down, when he broods in the prison of winter, shivering with indifference, biding his time, dreaming of an escape, of freedom, of April? I want to believe that he did, as I am looking for both sympathy and inspiration. Yet given the night we've had, Thoreau's optimism is starting to seem less useful.

I hear a loud, wooden clunk upstairs in Bennett and Abby's room. Bennett, who has rolled himself up in his wool blanket, has fallen out of his little bed. I find him on the floor still asleep: a seven-year-old mummy with a Pokémon tattoo on his cheek and a blue Wiffle Ball bat sticking out of the bedroll six inches from his head. He must have been holding it before he fell asleep and formed his wool cocoon. I pull the bat out and leave him asleep on the oak floor.

Carol has heard the bump too and also drifts into Bennett's room. Then she comes down into the kitchen. Was that a word that came out of her mouth? Now I recognize it: "Coffee." "Yeah," I say, "it's brewing." She squints at the digital stove clock: 6:20. We are both groggy, and look at each other with the quiet love and humor that such mornings require. Then we pour ourselves cups of coffee and get to work. I start to make the sandwiches—cutting and shuffling slices of wheat bread and smoked turkey and cheese like a short-order blackjack dealer. Carol gets the kids up and tries to sort out which one has chorus, which one is supposed to bring a packet of valentines, which one plays the flute, which one needs to review their multiplication flash cards (just the 8s and 9s), when and where basketball practice is being held, why there are only two pairs of boots for three pairs of feet by the door, and what she has done with the snacks she bought yesterday.

An hour or so later, the kids gather at the door around a colorful heap of coats and snow pants and gloves and hats. By now, we are running late. Bennett is certain Abby has stolen his gloves. Abby doesn't dispute this, which doesn't help. And she can't find her backpack. (That's because it's still sitting in the snow in the front yard—where she left it yesterday after school while talking to her friend). Tessa wants to know whether anyone has seen her cell phone and whether she can have two dollars for a raffle. I can't find my billfold, nor Carol her purse. Tessa digs eight quarters out of the coin bowl and runs out the door, hoping not to miss the bus. Carol hustles Bennett and Abby out the door and drops them off at school on her way to work.

And just like that the circus closes, and the house is quiet. Since it's Friday and I don't teach, I return to my desk, taking notes on Thoreau's winter delights. Another journal passage: "Alone in distant woods or fields . . . even in a bleak and, to most, cheerless day like this . . . I come to myself, I once more feel myself grandly related, and that cold and solitude are friends of mine."[5]

I admire the sentiment, the grand relation, but still don't quite trust his optimism—nor how he always finds it alone in the woods, rather than with people in town. I start to wonder whether it is the breadth of his life experience or the narrowness that lends him this resilient hope. And I remain curious about all that he doesn't say, about the life that didn't find its way into print. His deepest insights explore the formation of the individual rather than of human relationships or community.[6] Though I suppose it was his intense self-focus and the resulting self-knowledge that enabled his joyful solitude during the darkest months of the year.

But I have another theory about his stunning optimism, a provocative and poorly researched theory: what if Thoreau used St. John's wort—that "natural" antidepressant you can find today at any drugstore? He often mentions the plant, and it grows all around Walden Pond. What if he started each day with a few strong cups of St. John's wort tea and had a St. John's wort salad every evening, but never mentioned his addiction to its powerful healing properties in his books or journal?

I don't see it as a problem. After all, writers who take drugs to enhance their work are not like pro baseball players who take steroids to improve their batting averages. What great American writer was not addicted to something or other? And it hasn't seemed to diminish their work or careers. I guess I always assumed such vices were a tolerable balm against a writer's tortured self-absorption and unmet expectations. My point: were we to discover that Thoreau was dependent on St. John's wort to relieve his (yet unproven) spirals of depression, it would not harm his reputation as the first American nature writer. Quite the contrary—it would simply mean he was communing with nature on a much deeper level than anyone had previously thought.

There's only one problem with this theory. In Thoreau's time, St. John's wort was a general herbal "cure" used for a variety of illnesses: nervous disorders, gastric problems, uterine cramping, anemia, and worms. The most "reliable" antidepressant was whiskey. No one knew how the brain worked. Serotonin had not been discovered.

So, I confess—there's another reason I'm arguing that Thoreau was dependent on herbal antidepressants when there's no evidence to support it: I used to take Prozac and have known the ebb and flow of depression. I'm ashamed to admit it, really—that my comfortable life became so crowded and confusing for my anxious mind that I sometimes found myself lost in what became a familiar darkness. I tried St. John's wort, and long walks, and swimming, and a therapist, and it all helped. But not enough to see much light, or get back to where I thought I should be living: in gratitude—for the wonder of my family and friends and good coffee and hot showers.

Yet I resisted drugs for a long time, fearing what I'd never know: was it me who was thinking and loving and writing, or someone else—some artificially balanced drone whose passions had been doused, who had stopped searching? What of those great artists whose best work seems to stem from their emotional instability and addictions, who ride alternating waves of depression and euphoria toward artistic genius? There is one problem with this approach though, as Carol has reminded me: most of those people made shitty parents and partners.

So I finally went to see my doctor and told her I was depressed. She wrote me a prescription for the most commonly prescribed type of drug in America: an antidepressant. (Blood-pressure medication runs a close second.) I took Prozac for a few years, and it helped. I was less passionate but more productive. Less emotional but more focused. Less driven and more balanced.

Yet I also felt disappointed—like I wasn't strong enough, or like I was taking a drug to repair my personality rather than fend off a disease. What if the disease was only that—dis-ease—a deep uneasiness, a difficult sadness, that I had somehow been convinced was not tolerable? But sadness and grief are part of being human.

Though less and less so it seems—at least for Americans. One in ten of us now takes medication for depression. We like happy pills. And so do the drug and insurance companies. Pills are more profitable than therapy. And unlike therapy, we don't have to do anything except wait for the drug to work. Or so I thought. This morning I read a research study that claims that depressed patients on placebos improve 75 percent as often as those on real medication.[7] Wow. If sugar pills work as well as drugs, does that mean it really is "all in your head"?

I can just imagine Thoreau's response to all of this—to our get-happy culture, to our pharmaceutical solution to our lives of quiet desperation. He wouldn't be surprised to learn that as income levels have skyrocketed over the last fifty years, so has the rate of depression.[8] In *Walden*, he argues that even his affluent neighbors with the most modern conveniences—with "clean paint and paper, a Rumsford Fireplace, back plastering, Venetian blinds, a copper pump, and a commodious cellar" will not be truly happy until they understand what all that stuff requires of the owner. "[T]he cost of a thing," he later writes, "is the amount of what I will call life which is required to be exchanged for it, immediately or in the long run."[9]

This last line reminds me of a church group Carol and I were in several years ago. The quote appeared in the book the group was studying: *Your Money or Your Life*.[10] The author wrote that we all have a finite amount of "life," of time and energy, or what he called "life energy," and we have to decide how to "spend" it. The presumption was that we were all unknowingly trading quality time with friends and family, or with music and art, for material stuff we didn't need. We would be happier if we spent our money in a way that reflected our deepest values. And so we met every week and talked about how to make better choices so that we were less desperate and more deliberate: we would walk and ride bikes more and drive less, and shop in thrift stores, and recycle our own clothes and everything else we could, and share our power tools and do our own repairs, and grow more vegetables, and stay in better touch with our neighbors, and on and on. The word that kept coming up was *enough*. Like Thoreau, the book argues that less is more, that a happy life is a balanced one.

But after a few months the book group broke up. And without the anchor of those discussions, we drifted back into old patterns: our harried lives again became driven by convenience rather than conscience. Carol and I rarely discussed how to balance our time and our money, because we just didn't have time. We still live in that irony. And though we know that real happiness can't be purchased at a mega mall or on eBay, no one is immune from the multibillion-dollar media onslaught that constantly tries to argue the opposite.

I'm not always sure how to live toward *enough* within a culture of *more*. Though sometimes there are events that startle me back into trying. I clipped out a *Chicago Tribune* article about one of them last year. It was in November on the day after Thanksgiving—Black Friday—the biggest shopping day of the year. At five that morning, thirty-four-year-old Jdimytai Damour, who worked at the Walmart in Valley View, New York, was trampled to death by a herd of wild animals—suburban shoppers seeking sale prices. They burst through the door just before it was opened and knocked Mr. Damour down. Three other people were injured. It took a while to pull the body out because the throng of shoppers kept surging over it. When store officials decided to close the store due to the death, shoppers became irate and began yelling at management.

One can only imagine the depth of the emptiness, of the sadness, that must have driven those people to stampede. It seems that the whole point of thanksgiving, of gratitude, is trusting that you have enough right where you are, rather than always longing for more somewhere else—to choose a deliberate happiness rather than a desperate one.

I would like to learn how to do that—to recognize the gift of enough.

꒰

By early afternoon the day has grown dark and cloudy, but Thoreau, of course, hasn't. So I stop pretending that he's a St. John's wort addict. The bottom line is that though the guy sometimes repressed his grief, and was a bit cranky, he could also find joy in a drip of rain or the whisper of a pine bough. And he found it not just in the summer or spring, but in the freezing depth of winter. Which is maybe another clue to his deliberate happiness: perhaps it was not separate from sadness but balanced by it.

Maybe sadness doesn't deny happiness but defines it. Maybe the joy of the coming spring is rooted in the frozen tomb of winter, in the dark waiting for what the sadness will become. Which is where I am right now—waiting and looking out the kitchen window, seeking light at the end of the long tunnel of winter. But I see very little. Instead, the darkness is deep and spreading—down the street and around the trees and bushes. And now it's snowing. Or is that sleet? What a muddy, slushy mess. If it weren't so depressing, it would be funny.

I consider the line on the T-shirt I bought last year at Walden Pond: "What would Thoreau do?" My guess is he would walk straight into that awe-full winter muck—perhaps playing his flute at the same time. And somehow, he would be uplifted and inspired to write about all he has learned to see in the darkness.

I admire this wild joy, but I don't understand it. Darkness—in print or in person—has rarely felt like an invitation to me. I just don't work that way. And I'm not going out in that crappy weather. So I stay inside but keep an eye on the window. That's one of Thoreau's notions I do understand: "The necessity of being forever on the alert."[11] Sometimes good things can happen if you just keep watch. What we seek affects what we can see. So I try to see some light, and to believe that waiting for it is as sacred as its arrival, that patience itself is a kind of prayer.

A little while later, I spot Bennett's red coat and orange-and-blue Chicago Bears stocking cap rounding the corner a block away. Watching him walk that last block with his friend Blaise is a kind of solace for me, the kindling of a quiet gratitude I often lose. Bennett laughs and talks and sometimes wrestles with his friend. They both lie in the snow on their backs for a minute in our neighbors' yard and then pop up again and chase each other in circles like squirrels. Then they stop to make snowballs. When Bennett gets inside, he pulls one out of each pocket and hands them to me; they're hard and icy. "Let's put these in the freezer," he says, "and have a snowball fight in the summer when it's really hot." I help him pull his boots off, and we put the snowballs way in the back of the freezer. I make hot chocolate, and we sit at the kitchen table across from each other. We talk about how long we think the snowballs will last, whether it will snow again before spring, and all the things we want to do when summer comes.

Chapter 18

Traveling at Night
Seers and Seekers

Men talk about traveling . . . as if seeing were all in the eyes and a man could sufficiently report what he stood bodily before, when the seeing depends ever on the being.

HENRY DAVID THOREAU, *Journal*[1]

Last night, after the kids went to bed, I drove to the farm and arrived around midnight. I can usually find my way to the cabin in the darkness, because the opening in the trees above the pathway lets in soft splinters of star- or moonlight—just enough to make my way. But it was overcast. I found the entrance to the trail, took a few steps in, and then everything went black. As I crept slowly forward, I waved my hands out in front of me, searching for low tree limbs. I did the same with my feet, sliding them out in search of roots. I found one with my foot and assumed it was the next tree in line, marking the trail. So I took two steps forward (I thought— but what was "forward"?). A thick, wet pine bough smacked me in the face. A twig stabbed me in my left eye—a sharp jab between the top of my eyeball and the socket rim that nearly punctured my lid. Ow! This sent me stumbling off the path, staggering around in the dark. But finally, using my left hand to protect my face and my right as a probe, I felt my way back to the trail opening. There I paused and considered whether I should go back to the farmhouse for a flashlight.

And then I remembered something: this had happened before, and I had found my way. I took a deep, slow breath and stopped thinking, which helped orient me. My senses then somehow began to read the darkness, to perceive the opening in the blackness ahead of me. I stepped forward again, but more slowly and methodically this time. And though I could not sense the location of the large trees that lined the path, I could sense where they were not—their absence. So I kept walking. After thirty or so steps, I thought I was at the oak tree where a narrow path branches off at 90 degrees toward the cabin steps. But the trunk was too thick. I got it right the next time, turned, and walked into the porch. It was colder inside the cabin than out. Too tired to make a fire, I slept in my clothes in a sleeping bag.

ﻼ

When I awake this morning, my breath puffs out in clouds. I gather an armload of sticks, lay them in the iron stove, and grab a few logs from the woodpile to split. The weight and rhythm of the maul swinging in my hands feels good, like a pendulum, like I have become some sort of organic clock. I rip open time with the *THRUCK* of the heavy iron wedge, dividing a pine log into halves, and then *THRUCK* and *THRUCK*—into quarters. The hard, dull sound and sweet, bitter scent of that moment, of the newly split wood, drifts and diffuses through the air—marks time and then lets it go.

I return to the woodpile for more logs and see a fuzzy knot of orange in a gap and pull it out. It's a woolly bear—one of those fat, furry, two-inch-long black-and-orange caterpillars you always see in September eating themselves silly. He looks dead but is in a kind of suspended animation called diapause. Lowered temperatures and shortened days in October trigger the "pause." But when it warms up in May and the days lengthen, they awaken, eat, spin their cocoons, and emerge as tiger moths to flutter off into the meadow. A week or two later they lay their eggs and die. Then the eggs hatch into caterpillars and the cycle continues.

As I re-cover the woolly bear with another log, I can't help but wonder what it's like to spend half of your life waiting in the darkness. I know it's all instinct, that insects don't really "think." But the relativity of such a life—of time itself—startles me. The caterpillar's life seems much too brief. Yet his *present* is the same as mine—unending and fleeting.

The sappy pine pops and sizzles in the stove. It's dry, but unlike maple or oak burns dirty and smudges up the stove window. When the fire is blazing, I close down the damper in the flue to a crack to cut the oxygen and slow the burn. The riotous twists of flame magically diminish, both in height and velocity, as if they are suddenly moving in slow motion. I watch the fire thankfully, thinking of how my solitude here does the same thing—slows the burn of time.

I pull out *Walden* and turn to a passage that always comforts me:

> God himself culminates in the present moment, and will never be more divine in the lapse of all the ages. And we are enabled to apprehend at all what is sublime and noble only by the perpetual instilling . . . of the reality which surrounds us.[2]

Soon I am completely lost in the burning wood, in the prayers of ash and smoke, of darkness and light. And it is then, for just a little while, that a prayer is answered. Amid the flame and flicker, I ride the orange-and-red river of time until I can *see*. What I see has no words. If I had to reduce it to language, I might use Thoreau's: "the gospel of this moment"—the *good news* that the present is eternal and part of one timeless Belonging.

By noon the cabin is boiling and my shirt is drenched in sweat. I crack a window, get some water, and return to *Walden*. As I skim through my notes, I can't help but notice how often the words *travel* and *traveler* turn up. This interests me, because Thoreau usually stayed close to home. Many know his famous line, "I have traveled a good deal in Concord." But fewer know the line that follows: "and everywhere, in shops, and offices, and fields, the inhabitants have appeared to me to be doing penance."[3]

His point: the "penance" of material obligation, or "making a living," can prevent the deepest kind of travel—a wild, inward journey, which leads not to a place but to a way of seeing. Both seeing and seeking are essential to the traveler. Thoreau reiterates this idea in his books and his *Journal*, and I much admire it. Enough so that most of this book is a humble attempt to find meaning in my own "travels" on home ground, from the wilds of suburban Chicago to the woods and farms of southwest Michigan.

Yet traveling further afield—visiting different cultures and countries—can also teach the traveler much about themselves and their home. Were Thoreau alive today, my guess is that he would be just as committed to Concord's natural history. But given the relative ease of travel, he might also decide to wander further from familiar terrain.

❧

This winter, aside from my local jaunts, I made a two-week trip to Nicaragua as part of a Witness for Peace[4] delegation with a dozen students from Ohio University. But it was also a journey into the wilds of memory. Twenty-five years ago, I too was a college student wanting to do something about U.S. foreign policy besides going to demonstrations. So, in 1985, I turned down a high school teaching job and went to Nicaragua to see a revolution with my own eyes.

A naïve, small-town Iowa kid, I arrived in Managua in the

middle of a guerrilla war to find the entire city surrounded by tanks. I spent that summer learning how to see a culture so foreign to me, so impoverished and unpredictable, so inspiring and wondrous, that at times it was more than my eyes could hold. But I kept them open—to the sweating brown faces peering through the dusty heat, to the farmers whacking green sugar cane with their shiny *bolos,* to the rumble of tanks and the locking and loading of rifles, to the tinny melodies of guitars, to the rats scuttling along the rafters above me at night, to the flies buzzing around rotten meat in the market, and later, buzzing around a slain child's body at a funeral mass, a child from the barrio where I was living. And they didn't dress or try to hide the nickel-size hole in his throat.

I can still see it, and everything else from all those long-ago trips, even though I'm now almost fifty and live a more settled life. And yes, I've noticed—we still haven't saved the world or anything else. Wars are still raging. Most of the people on this planet are still poor, their central concern food and shelter. And most of the rest of us still act as if we can't see them, as if we aren't related. Which is why this return trip to Nicaragua with this band of students—as we talked with political leaders and *maquila* workers and trash pickers and farmers—felt like a sacred moment of re-vision.

On the last day with the group in Managua, Brian and I walked from our guesthouse over to a gas station to get cigarettes and pop. Brian was a student I had talked with some, but never very personally. During the walk he told me he had just finished his BA, was doing an MA in Spanish, but lately he had been feeling unsettled. "I'm getting older," he said. "And I'm still not sure what I should be doing with my life, what I'm searching for."

I was taken aback, as I wasn't expecting, at that moment, to hear the theme song of my own life. "I've been trying to answer that question for the last twenty-five years." I said. "Still no good answers. That's why I came on this trip. I thought *you* were going to tell *me.*"

He laughed at this, looking both amused and relieved. Then he told me about the family he stayed with in San Ramón, a remote village we had just visited for three days. He showed me a passage from his journal:

Carlos, the son of the woman I'm living with, visited today. He was sitting outside, so I introduced myself. I discovered we were both the same age: 23. After some small talk I asked him what he did for fun in the campo. "Sobrevivir," he said. "Estoy tratando de sobrevivir." ("I'm trying to survive.") I kind of wish I hadn't asked. I felt guilty telling him what I did. He had no idea about my life. Then I noticed him looking at my shiny blue maglite. It was worth much more to him than me. I wanted to give it to him, and everything else I had: my sleeping bag, shoes, shorts, pants, another jacket. That isn't allowed, but still, I felt uneasy and unsure how to connect with him.

"*Sobrevivir.* What could I say to that?" Brian asked as we crossed the dusty highway to the convenience store. "How could I respond? What do I do with such a word?"

"Carry it with you," is all I could think of to say. I told him that my first trip to Nicaragua felt like three months of wandering around in the dark. I wanted to do something—to try to end the war, and the poverty—but I finally learned that the best thing I could do was listen. And surprisingly, I too encountered a young Nicaraguan named Carlos, who challenged my thinking and gave me a story to carry.

OCOTAL, NICARAGUA
MAY 1985
We were sitting in a café sipping warm Victoria beer and eating cold rice and beans when Carlos put his finger to his ear. "Escuche," he said. "Bombas."

He looked toward the north. I listened intently. I had heard

the same faint irregular thunder coming from the mountains the
night before. But I had thought it was thunder. Now I was a
little scared. The bombs seemed so close. I was glad I was
returning to Managua in the morning.

Carlos was also leaving in the morning—for his battalion in
the mountains. He was on his monthly two-day leave. Three days
before, a contra mortar had blown some shrapnel into his right
forearm. He had wrapped a piece of shirt around it, but it didn't
do any good. The wound was blue and brown and still seeping.
It hurt to look at it.

He looked young in his baggy Sandinista greens and worn
high-top tennis shoes. Or maybe he just didn't look like a
soldier—like he could do what soldiers were supposed to do. Yet
he didn't look or talk like a teenager, either. He wanted to know
why the U.S. was trying to overthrow his country, why he had to
defend his right to "rice and beans and hope," why his father and
brother had died doing that. Why did he have to hug an AK-47
in the mountains in the rain instead of his girlfriend in the
moonlight in Léon?

It was hard for me to understand Carlos's fluid Spanish. But
even harder when it started to rain. The rhythmic pinging on the
corrugated steel roof gradually grew into a relentless machine-
gunning—so loud I had to yell when asking Carlos what they did
for protection during this season in the mountains. "Nothing," he
yelled back. "We have a lean-to and tents, but you still get wet,
and sick."

I kept trying to listen, but the rain and beer had weakened
my concentration and I found myself wondering what Carlos,
a good-looking seventeen-year-old, would be doing right now if
he were in the U.S. Playing tennis and golf and video games
and going to homecoming? Learning how to drive and play the
piano and working on computers? He'd have more than "rice
and beans and hope" anyway. Or maybe not. He talked about
freedom with a passion I didn't quite understand.

Around nine, the rain eased back to a steady pinging, which made it easier to talk. But Carlos said he had to go. Absent-mindedly, I asked him if he didn't want to wait for the rain to stop. "Until August?" he said. We both laughed. I offered him my old black pop-up umbrella. He took it. Then he grabbed his AK-47, opened the umbrella, and walked off into the dripping darkness.[5]

The next morning I was thinking about that darkness, and the gift of Carlos's story, and of travel itself, as I helped Brian and the group load the bus for their trip to the airport. I said my good-byes and thanked them for letting me travel with them. The bus pulled away, and I already missed them, their passion and idealism. Enough so that I soon began to wonder where my own had gone in these intervening years since I had first visited Nicaragua.

Was it really *twenty-five years* ago? What, I wondered (and feared), have I actually been *doing* all these years? How did I lose all that time? Had I somehow been living the robotic penance that Thoreau warned against? Or was I was more like the caterpillar in the woodpile, sometimes slipping into a kind of diapause—waiting in the darkness for something else, something better, for the moment I would become what I was supposed to be?

But Brian and Carlos reminded me: we don't really know what we're supposed to be, because we never stop becoming something new. That was Thoreau's point: we never stop waking up. The present is all there is, and it never feels like arrival.

❧

I had three days to visit old haunts after the group left. On my last day, I visited the city of Granada. I still don't know what I was looking for, but I'm thankful for what I found:

GRANADA, NICARAGUA

DECEMBER 2007

I am walking along Lake Granada alone when a wiry teenager in a ragged T-shirt and jeans comes up to me smiling, with his hand extended. I thought for sure he'd ask me for money. "Me llamo Gilberto. Y no quiero dinero." Gilberto says he doesn't want money. I don't believe him. He says he wants to tell the story of the Lake Granada flood, and of all the people that died. If I want to give him something afterward, that would be fine, but I didn't need to. Before I can respond, he launches in—the waves were twenty feet high, dozens were killed, hundreds of boats and homes destroyed . . .

I ask him to stop, and tell him I really just want to take a walk. He looks heartbroken and slinks away. I'm surprised he gives up so easily. He intrigues me. I've never seen anyone try to sell a story on the street before. But I didn't want to lead him on. A half-dozen people had already stopped me, either simply begging, or wanting to sell hammocks or paintings or jewelry. I'm not good at saying no, but saying yes turns you into a magnet for anyone selling anything. The guilt wears me down. I hate feeling like a tourist.

"Tourists don't know where they've been. Travelers don't know where they're going," Paul Theroux once wrote.[6] I like the contrast. But while I may think of myself as a traveler, Gilberto reminds me that they, too, are defined by their privilege.

About an hour later I finish my walk. On my way back to the hostel, I pass the old cathedral. Mass is in session, and out on the stone ledge I see Gilberto. He waves. When I'm within twenty yards, he motions for me to come to him. I reluctantly walk over. "Pan," he says, "pan." Bread. He has his hands out, turned skyward. Suddenly he doesn't look so healthy. I feel awful. "OK," I say.

We cross the street to a pulpería. The old woman behind the iron bars of the large window smiles at me. She understands. I get two big bags of her fresh rolls. "What else?" I ask Gilberto. He looks confused. "What would you like to put on the bread?" I continue in my broken Spanish. He scans the rows of cans and jars on the few shelves behind the counter and points to a large, red tin of sardines. The lady holds it up as if to ask whether this is what he wants. "Sí, esto. Sí, esto," Gilberto says. He seems way too excited about this, and I'm feeling a bit uneasy. "Ay, tan rico, tan rico," he says over and over with such an odd mix of joy and disbelief that when his eyes tear up, mine do too. And then I finally got it. He's hungry. Really hungry. "Es como un regalo de Navidad," he says. For him, the food is "like a Christmas present."

He takes the bread and sardines in the plastic bag and looks at me like I have done some great thing, like I've performed a miracle. But all I'm trying to do is to learn how to see in the dark, to see what matters—to see the gift that he's offering me.

"Adiós," he says, and puts both hands on his heart. But he does not mean "Good-bye." He means "To God" ("a Dios"). In Nicaragua, this phrase is used as a greeting, whether coming or going, and as a blessing. Then Gilberto offers me some of the bread. "No, thanks," I say. We shake hands, and he walks off.

Ten minutes later I arrive at my hostel, and there is an old, humped man begging outside. I have to pass by him to enter. He is blind, and his large hands are cupped together to form a kind of grizzled brown collection plate. Clearly startled, he smiles when he feels my five-córdoba coin drop in his palm. "Gracias a Dios," he says. "Gracias a Dios." I like this. I like that he can't see me, and that he is thanking God, who perhaps he can see.

❧

A branch near the cabin crashes down in the wind. The crack and the thud call me back to the present, and to how far I have traveled into these stories, into the time made by wood and fire. How odd it is tonight to think of that old blind man and Gilberto, and Brian and Carlos, and my own college years, all as I sit alone in the darkness in a cabin in the woods. The memories dredge up all kinds of conflicting emotions—from gratitude and joy to regret and disappointment. I turn a lamp on, set some water on the stove for tea, and open Thoreau's *Journal*. After skimming a few pages, I find the passage I'm looking for:

> "A traveler! I love his title," Thoreau writes. "A traveler is to be reverenced as such. His profession is the best symbol of our life. Going from _____ toward _____; it is the history of every one of us. I am interested in those that travel at night."[7]

I fill in the blanks: going from wood toward fire, from tomorrow toward now, from darkness toward light—and back again. I like his choice of *toward* rather than *to,* implying direction rather than destination. He is interested in those who travel in the darkness. But for him, darkness and light are not absolutes, nor opposites. And thankfully, neither are seeing and seeking.

Chapter 19

Slow Pilgrim
Walking and Praying

Some of my townsmen . . . can remember, and have described
to me some walks which they took ten years ago, in which they
were so blessed as to lose themselves for half an hour in the
woods; but I know very well they have confined themselves to
the highway ever since. . . .

HENRY DAVID THOREAU[1]

Sunday. I tramp down a muddy path through the woods toward
the river. Some of the wildflowers have already bloomed—the
bloodroot and spring beauties. The trout lilies and Solomon's seal
and red trillium will likely be early, too—in a week or so. And it's
oddly warm for the first day of April: 62 degrees. Like many states,
Michigan has season creep—spring keeps arriving earlier due to
global warming. The state climatologist says the mean temperature
is now 2 degrees higher than it was in 1980. Botanists around the
state report that plants and trees are budding and blooming earlier
this year than any other on record. And the warmth also, of course,
affects bird migration and mating, which is why I've come to the
farm for the afternoon. Dan e-mailed a few days ago that the great
blue herons had returned. I want to welcome them back.

When I get within a hundred feet of the herons' sycamore, I hear the low, familiar cackles and look up to see only two repaired nests. The other three nests are weather-beaten, full of holes, clearly unoccupied. Three heron pairs didn't come back this year. And half of the birds on the other side of the river didn't come back, either. It's hard to say why, but it saddens me and makes the two huge, gangly birds I'm watching through my binoculars all the more beautiful. They fidget in their nests for several minutes, moving sticks here and there with their long beaks. But finally one bird spots me, moves to the branchy precipice, makes his gawky, squawky liftoff, and falls into his slow, pumping rhythm. Not wanting to spook the other bird, I leave too, and continue along the river.

Since I still have a couple of hours, I decide to take a long walk before returning to my own wild nest and the chaos of a Monday morning. I've been trying to walk more lately. Here and at home. The simple rhythm of breath and body helps calm my anxious mind. Carol and I often walk these woods. And in the summer, we like to stroll through our neighborhood at dusk—when the dying light awakens new colors in the trees and softens the hard edges of the rooflines.

I began to care more about walking a few years ago when I first read Thoreau's essay "Walking." And the piece is so full of insight that I just keep returning to it. Thoreau walked for three or four hours every afternoon for much of his life and claimed he couldn't stay physically and intellectually balanced, or write, if he didn't. Though nobody I know can commit half their workday to walking, his insights are helpful. And reading the essay is kind of like taking a good walk.

He begins with two etymological definitions of the word *saunter*.[2] The first is *à la Sainte Terre,* or "to the holy land," suggesting pilgrims on their way to a holy place—as in the *Canterbury Tales* or the Hajj to Mecca. His second definition is from *sans terre,* or "without land."[3] He takes "without land" to mean without a home, claiming that the saunterer, or walker, in his homelessness, is at home anywhere, and *present* everywhere. I like these ideas: the "holy land" the walker seeks is not a faraway place, or even a place at all, but a way of seeing and loving the world, of being at home wherever you are.

As I walk along the river's oxbow, everything is waking from the dead—pushing through the brown bed of decay, rising up green toward the fire of the sun, which is casting its warm spokes of light here and there through the pines and budding oaks. The pools of sunlight on the ground sparkle and shiver like they are bits of the very spirit of the place—small oracles of light and dirt flickering with sentient wisdom. But by the time I reach the edge of the woods, they have all been swallowed by shadow, by a bank of cloud.

I walk out into the open meadow and think I see a red-tailed hawk kiting in the cool air. But when I look closer, the shivering V and tilty-fingered wings mark a turkey vulture scanning for carrion—the most common of birds, the unloved garbageman of the Midwestern sky. Who loves a bird that stands for death and decay? It is the antithesis of a state bird. No university sports team will ever choose the turkey vulture as its mascot. The cheerleaders would have to think of chants that rhyme with *scavenge*.

The drifting vulture reminds me of a scene on the beach last summer. One afternoon I stumbled on a clutch of screeching ring-billed gulls, which I assumed were bickering over a half-eaten bag of french fries or Doritos someone had dropped. But when I approached the loose ring of white birds, each one lifted into the air and peeled off into the wind, their wings flapping mirrors of sunlight in retreat. The object of their attention: a huge, black vulture ripping out the gut of a decaying coho salmon. Preoccupied with eating, the vulture wouldn't leave the fish until I could almost touch his oily feathers and smell his bloodied head. And he was back on the carcass after I had retreated only a few steps.

It was a brutal sight but not a brutal act. After all, the vulture does what it's made to do, what it's good at—cleaning up the mess. As I think of that gory scene now and track the dark form of the bird circling above me, I can't help but wonder what I was made to do—what people are for—and why it sometimes seems so unclear. I must have taken a half-dozen courses in grad school and seminary where my professors tried to teach me what it means to be human, what *human* being is. Each had his own answer. Though the best answer for me would come much later. And rather than separate people from other animals, it would blur the difference. It was the births of our children—that stunning reminder of our common physiology, that just like cats and horses, we are pushed from a warm body of water called mother. We too arrive here wet and squirming, dazed and innocent. To be human is to be animal.

Which I think is why I was so fascinated by what I discovered in a field guide I had just bought at a garage sale: *The Audubon Field Guide to North American Mammals.* While skimming through the book this morning at our kitchen table, I found an entry I hadn't even imagined: *Homo sapiens.* The species that writes the book *about* the animals includes itself in the book *as* an animal? I admired the biological humility, but it seemed we should be in a guide that includes our closest ancestors—the chimpanzees and gorillas. Though this *is* a North American guide, so it also makes sense. And there is one other primate listed in North America: the rhesus monkey.

I tried to imagine what the author would say about our habitat: "The human is often encountered in family groups in the evenings in ranch-style homes or high-rise apartments, but in daylight can be found alone—resting or grazing or texting—often in office buildings or shopping malls." And what about diet? "The human is an omnivore and eats a widely varied diet, ranging from raw vegetables and fruits to microwave dinners. Most human offspring will eat at least a few McDonald's Happy Meals during the preadolescent stage (6–10 years)." And what about breeding? "Like other primates, humans often mate for life, but unlike other primates, they typically initiate contact with prospective mates through Internet dating sites (which helps ensure compatibility and thus viable offspring)."

The entry for *Homo sapiens* actually didn't say anything about our habitat or diet or breeding. And there were no photos, as with the other mammals, just a generic drawing of a white naked guy and gal—like one of those body-part posters from elementary school. All they really included was a basic definition:

> Homo sapiens *(Latin for "knowing man") are the only living members of the Homo genus of bipedal primates in the great ape family. Their complex brains are capable of abstract reasoning, language, and introspection. This mental capability, combined with an erect body carriage that frees the hands for manipulating objects, has allowed humans to make far greater use of tools than other primates. Humans are also uniquely adept at utilizing systems of communication for self-expression and the exchange of ideas. They are noted for their desire to understand and influence their environment, seeking to explain and manipulate natural phenomena through science, philosophy, mythology, and religion.*

I presume the authors are trying to make a point: we too belong to the environment even as we are destroying it.[4] But in another way, that makes no sense. Grizzly bears and wolves don't read Audubon field guides. People do. So why is such a basic entry even necessary?

This paradox lingers in my large, highly developed brain as I continue on my erect bipedal way, traipsing through the warm, sunny meadow to one of the rough-hewn benches and poetry boxes Dan built a few years ago. The boxes are my favorite of Dan's many carpentry projects at the farm. Poetry. What could be more human? There are six of the benches and boxes on the farm, each placed along a different walking trail. They are a physical reminder to stop and attend—to a poem, or a tree, to the words in the woods. Dan made the benches out of huge split logs. And each sixteen-by-twenty-inch wooden box is mounted on a small post a few feet from the bench. The stained plywood boxes look like lecture podiums and have hinged lids that flip open to hold one book of poetry, a journal, and a pen. We put the books and journals into Tupperware containers, because it turns out that bugs like poetry too. Some spiders spent the winter nestled with Pablo Neruda in the poetry box near the oxbow. A caterpillar I know, however, prefers Carl Sandburg and the box beneath the apple tree.

But when I flip up the lid of the meadow box, I remember: the paper wasps love Mary Oliver. Last summer, when I opened this box, a dozen of her devotees tried to scare me away from their literary queen, and one stung me. Today, however, there are only two wasps, and they're still in cold-weather stupor and just want to be left alone. They stay in their cracks while I pull out the book *Why I Wake Early*. I've read it before yet am always drawn to one poem: "Where Does the Temple Begin, Where Does It End?"

Oliver's poetry is religious to me in that basic, essential way that Thoreau is religious: they both *tie together again* the human being and the natural world. Both remind me that we are created and related—in brain and breath, and birth and death. And like Thoreau, Oliver suggests that "worship" is about seeing and seeking.

Given Oliver's temple image, I suddenly imagine the poetry box as a little pulpit. So I walk up, stand behind it, and read her poem aloud to the captive community. This includes the committed natives: a red oak sapling, a budding sumac, and a patch of bluestem grass. But it also includes the weedy outsiders that are trying to take over: the garlic mustard, buckthorn, and multiflora rose.

WHERE DOES THE TEMPLE BEGIN, WHERE DOES IT END?

There are things you can't reach. But
you can reach out to them, and all day long.

The wind, the bird flying away. The idea of God.

And it can keep you as busy as anything else, and happier.

The snake slides away; the fish jumps, like a little lily,
out of the water and back in; the goldfinches sing
      from the unreachable top of the tree.

I look; morning to night I am never done with looking.

Looking I mean not just standing around, but standing around
      as though with your arms open.

And thinking: maybe something will come, some
      shining coil of wind,
         or a few leaves from any old tree—
            they are all in this too.

And now I will tell you the truth.
Everything in the world
comes.

At least, closer.

And, cordially.

Like the nibbling, tinsel-eyed fish; the unlooping snake.
Like goldfinches, little dolls of gold
fluttering around the corner of the sky

of God, the blue air.

No one responds to my scripture reading. No nodding or swaying. No one sends out an affirming leaf or a confetti of seeds. So next I try a silent prayer—the kind that can go on forever. Perhaps if I wait long enough the pastor and the rest of the congregation will arrive.

They don't. But the liturgy continues: a honking Canada goose rises in the silence, along with the hollow mechanical rapping of a woodpecker, and the wind whooshing up through the soft whorls of the white pines. Then comes confession: the hard, grinding whir of a chain saw, and the sad drone of the semitrucks roaring down the interstate. Overhead, a jet slowly draws a white line across the blue-gray bowl of the sky as it carries two hundred people to some place they need to arrive very soon. I wonder where they're all going.

Then the latecomers arrive. Two robins drop in just below me and peck around for bugs. An anthill stirs—three black ants called to duty by the sunlight. A small cloud of gnats appears, hovering near the bench. Their whiny anthem has three notes.

Then, finally, the pastor shows up: a wild turkey, which I must have startled, comes sprinting out of the woods all bothered and anxious, like a character from an old Disney cartoon. He pauses on the edge of the meadow looking crazy—like he's both terrified and wants to scold me—then tears back into the trees without giving his sermon.

Twenty minutes later comes the offering—or maybe it's communion: a red-tailed hawk appears, soaring high above our odd little church. A red-tail—four feet of wing, three pounds of blood and muscle, and with binoculars for eyes—can spot a mouse from a mile away. He can see if there are eggs in the wren's nest just above my head. And he can tell right now if my eyes are closed or opened. Though when I look up at him, I can't see anything clearly—except the wind, which he makes visible.

Soon the sun dips under a cloud and the hawk's slow, gliding shadow disappears from the weeds. Then a choir of mosquitoes hums the closing hymn. This is when the hawk breaks his circle and drifts away. His beak becomes the curved tip of a wide, strong-winged arrow pointing toward home. The benediction.

I leave the pulpit, walk to the end of the meadow, and turn onto a trail that loops around the pine forest and then follows the outer edge of our land. I cross into the neighbor's woods and just keep walking. I walk through another network of trails, which finally ends in a forty-acre cornfield. Tramping through the muddy husks and cobs, I soon reach a small vineyard and follow a long, lovely row of Concord grapevines until I reach a gravel road, Wee-Chik, which I follow until I reach Minnich Road, which winds back over the Galien River.

I don't know where I'm going. I just want to walk. Or maybe to pray, as that's how the best walks seem, like an emptying and opening. Today, as contrived as it may sound, I'm *trying* to lose track of time and self—to let go of my intellectual coordinates for a while and belong to the walk, to something bigger. It first happened when I was walking on the beach a long time ago. One minute I was worrying about how we'd pay our property taxes, and the next I was focused on my breath and had let go. My mind became as thought-less and rhythmic and fluid as the cool waves that rinsed my feet. And when I was done walking, I felt restored, in balance, as if I belonged right where I was.

That didn't quite happen today. I feel more emptied than opened. But that's all right. I am a slow and bungling pilgrim. One who now needs to pack his bag and get on the road. It's late. I sweep the cabin out and bring my stuff to the car. Both relieved and a bit sad to be heading home, I start down Flynn Road toward the interstate. The sun is half above and half below the horizon. I roll my windows down and get lost in that brief moment between night and day that belongs to neither. A flock of birds, warblers, are singing from a power line that crosses the road. I stop for a moment to listen. Since birds migrate in the deep of night, I wonder if they'll also be traveling tonight.

All around me the darkness is pushing back the light, but the light wants to linger. The road is lined with pine trees and in full shadow, except for one small gap, where a yellow stripe glows across the road. It takes ten seconds to drive through the town of Sawyer and a minute to reach the interstate, where I accelerate and merge into the growing darkness with hundreds of other cars, which are all whizzing and weaving around me on their way toward home.

Later, when I smell the steelworks of Gary, Indiana, I look out my window and see that a little piece of the sky has cleared—just a few stars, but they are radiant against the blackness. I try to count them, and then to imagine that little flock of warblers, which may be up there right now, flapping away—homing—migrating along the lakeshore to nesting grounds some of them have never seen. I wonder how they came to know the darkness so well, and what their other markers are, and whether they are tired or excited, and if those few stars encouraged them, and how they'll know for sure when they've arrived.

I call home on the cell, and Bennett answers.

"Hi, Daddy. Hey, guess what. The Sox are on, and I think they're going to win. It's 3 to 1. Where are you?"

"Hi, Benzo. I'm almost home. Is Mom there?"

"She took Abby to soccer."

"OK. Tell her I'll be there in an hour. See you soon."

"Good. Oh, and we won our soccer game—*and* we had malts and popcorn for supper."

"Wow. What a great night!"

"Yeah. OK. Bye, Daddy."

"Bye."

A half hour later, at the Chicago city limit, the traffic slows and tightens around me. There is no longer any open land or view of the lake, and oddly, very little darkness. I drive and brake and honk and pray toward home at thirty miles per hour on Interstate 290. The river of cars, of headlights and belching exhaust pipes, cuts through a canyon made by apartments and brick bungalows and box stores and ten-story parking garages. I imagine the coyotes and raccoons and geese out there in that same wilderness. While they hunt and prowl and sleep, I just keep following my low beams, and the red glow of the taillights, slowly humming toward home. Which I'm now hoping can be wherever you are, with whomever you love. That if you can see it, and them, then the holy land can be here, now. And you are always in the temple.

Acknowledgments

Thanks to the talented staff at Beacon Press for the remarkable care they put into making books, and especially to my editor, Alexis Rizzuto, for her encouragement, incisive reading, and editorial finesse.

Thanks to John Price for his thoughtful critique of the manuscript in its early stages, and to the other kind writers who provided feedback: Deborah Adelman, Tammie Bob, Cindy Crosby, Stuart Dybek, Roberta Gates, Renny Golden, David McGrath, April Nauman, Robert Root, Steve VanderStaay, Valerie Weaver-Zercher, and Liz Whiteacre.

Thanks to Jeffrey Cramer, curator at the Thoreau Institute, for his generous assistance with my questions regarding Thoreau's life and work, and to Michael Frederick and Tom Potter, at the Thoreau Society, for their insights on this project and their hard work to keep Thoreau's ideas vibrant in the twenty-first century.

Thanks to the following institutions and foundations: the College of DuPage, in Glen Ellyn, Illinois, for a sabbatical leave; the University of Iowa Nonfiction Writing Program, for a fellowship to write at La Muse, in Aude, France; the Chicago Theological Seminary and the Henry Luce Foundation, for a residency at the seminary; the National Endowment for the Humanities, for a research seminar in Concord, Massachusetts; the Lily Foundation and the Collegeville Institute for Ecumenical and Cultural Research, in Collegeville, Minnesota, for time at the institute; the Morton Arboretum (and its faculty), in Lisle, Illinois, for superb instruction in the field and classroom; and the Dekoven Center, in Racine, Wisconsin, for offering a quiet place to write and pray.

Thanks to my core mentors: Claude Marie Barbour, Luna Dingayan, Chuck Jorgensen, Carl Klaus, Richard Lloyd-Jones, Bob Majerus, Cleo Martin, and David Wilson. And to a mentor-in-print: Scott Russell Sanders, whose many books helped me find a voice as a writer, and remain a source of insight and solace.

Thanks to the many teachers and coaches who so generously share in the care and mentoring of our children, and to the other friends and colleagues who contributed to this project in a variety of ways: John Dagger, Jason Ertz, Beverly Reed, and all the members of Covenant Farm.

Finally, thanks to my family, whose support I have come to rely on: my parents-in-law, my mom and dad, and my brothers. But my deepest thanks go to Carol. Her resilient love is the locus of all I understand as *home*. This book would not have been possible without her patience and generosity. And to Tessa, Abby, and Bennett: you are my north star, the wild, steadfast light that marks my way. I love you.

Notes

Epigraph
1. Henry David Thoreau, *I to Myself: An Annotated Selection from the Journal of Henry D. Thoreau,* ed. Jeffrey S. Cramer (New Haven, CT: Yale University Press, 2007), 86.

Deliberate Life
1. Thoreau, *I to Myself,* 89.
2. Henry David Thoreau, *Walden: A Fully Annotated Edition,* ed. Jeffrey S. Cramer (New Haven, CT: Yale University Press, 2004), 68.
3. Ibid., 170. The land around Walden Pond was not wilderness but a conventional woodlot when purchased by Ralph Waldo Emerson. Thoreau himself writes, "The scenery of Walden is on a humble scale."

SPRING

1. Thoreau, *Walden,* 317.

Chapter 1: Picking Blackberries
1. Thoreau, *Walden,* 96.
2. Ibid., 113.
3. Ibid., 90.
4. Joanne Vining, Melinda Merrick, and Emily Price, "The Distinction Between Humans and Nature: Human Perceptions of Connectedness to Nature and Elements of the Natural and Unnatural," *Human Ecology Review* 15, no. 1 (2008): 1–11.

Chapter 2: In Plain Sight
1. Thoreau, *I to Myself,* 13.
2. This is likely due less to local residents' disinterest in water quality than to socioeconomics. Many who live in the Galien basin could not afford to replace or repair their faulty septic systems.

3. Henry David Thoreau, *Letters to a Spiritual Seeker,* ed. Bradley P. Dean (New York: Norton, 2005), 183.

Chapter 3: Fathers Watching Sons
1. Thoreau, *Walden,* 94.
2. Ibid., 303.

Chapter 4: Saunter
1. Henry David Thoreau, *Excursions* (London: Anthem, 2007), 106.
2. Thoreau, *Walden,* 221.
3. Ibid., 220–21.
4. Bert Hölldobler and Edward O. Wilson, *Journey to the Ants: A Story of Scientific Exploration* (Boston: Belknap Press of the Harvard University Press, 1998), 123.
5. Quoted by Robert D. Richardson, *Henry Thoreau: A Life of the Mind* (Berkeley: University of California Press, 1988), 115.

Chapter 5: The Gay Cardinal
1. Thoreau, *Walden,* 82.
2. Marilyn Muszalski Shy, "Interspecific Feeding Among Birds: A Review," *Journal of Field Ornithology* 53, no. 4 (1982): 370–93.
3. Mark Bekoff, *The Emotional Life of Animals: A Leading Scientist Explores Animal Joy, Empathy, and Sorrow and Why They Matter* (Auburn, CA: New World, 2007), 33.

SUMMER

1. Thoreau, *I to Myself,* 322.

Chapter 6: Cabin Fever
1. Thoreau, *Walden,* 129.
2. Thoreau, *I to Myself,* 87.
3. Thoreau, *Walden,* 127.
4. There are several other possible origins of the term—including the anxiety caused by confinement in a ship's cabin during the long passage from Europe to America.
5. Thoreau, *Excursions,* 105. This phrase seems to borrow from Emerson's early essay "Nature," which refers to people being "part and particle of nature"—a central idea of transcendentalism.

6. Thoreau, *Walden,* 162.
7. Ibid., 88.
8. Ibid., 127.
9. Ibid., 128.

Chapter 7: In the Time of the Cicada

1. Henry David Thoreau, *The Journal of Henry David Thoreau,* eds. Bradford Torrey and F. H. Allen, 7 vols. (New York: Dover, 1962), 197.

Chapter 8: Mushrooms

1. Thoreau, *Journal,* 479.
2. Pieces from his *Journal* were published first in four seasonal volumes prepared by Harrison Gray Otis Blake: *Early Spring in Massachusetts* (1881), *Summer* (1884), *Winter* (1888), and *Autumn* (1892). In 1906, Houghton Mifflin published a fourteen-volume edition.
3. Thoreau, *I to Myself,* 286.
4. Ibid., 287.
5. Thoreau's deep emotional connection to his brother is also suggested by his developing a sympathetic case of lockjaw after John's death. This condition kept him in bed for a month and led to a depression that lasted much longer. See Philip Cafaro, *Thoreau's Living Ethics: Walden and the Pursuit of Virtue* (Athens: University of Georgia Press, 2006), 231.
6. Thoreau, *I to Myself,* 113.
7. Ibid., 115.
8. According to Thoreau scholar Walter Harding, there is no evidence that he was physically intimate with men or women, yet his "actions and words . . . indicate a specific sexual interest in members of his own sex." See Walter Harding, "Thoreau's Sexuality," *Journal of Homosexuality* 21, no. 3 (1991): 23–45.
9. In November 1856, Thoreau visited Walt Whitman in New York City. Thoreau was enamored with Whitman and the raw, honest ramble of his poetry, but he also seemed uneasy with its sexual directness. He was likely aware of Whitman's homoeroticism—in person and in print—but wrote little about it. The visit is mentioned in one of Thoreau's letters to his friend Harrison Gray Otis Blake in Thoreau, *Letters to a Spiritual Seeker,* 143–44.
10. Thoreau, *I to Myself,* 138–39.
11. Thoreau, *Journal,* 1136.

Chapter 9: Lake Glass

1. Thoreau, *Excursions,* 166.
2. Also called beach glass or mermaid's tears, or sea glass when found near an ocean, where it is more common and produced more quickly due to the saline quality of the water and to the stronger surf.
3. And, given the catastrophic British Petroleum oil spill in the Gulf of Mexico in 2010, one can only imagine how quickly a significant spill or leak at the BP refinery in Whiting, Indiana, would devastate the lake's ecological balance.
4. Thoreau, *Letters to a Spiritual Seeker,* 72. This is from a September 1852 letter to Harrison Gray Otis Blake, a frequent correspondent and a Thoreau disciple.

Chapter 10: A Box of Wind

1. Thoreau, *Walden,* 82.
2. Henry David Thoreau, *A Week on the Concord and Merrimack Rivers* (Whitefish, MT: Kessinger, 2004), 98.
3. Thoreau, *Journal,* 1342.
4. I have not been able to find this paragraph anywhere else in Thoreau's work. However, because it was found in the original draft of "Walking," it is likely he included it when he presented the essay in public.
5. From page 95 of the original handwritten manuscript, which is located in the Concord Free Public Library in Concord, Massachusetts.
6. Emerson's essay "Nature" (1836) is often viewed as the philosophical launching of the transcendentalist movement.
7. Ralph Waldo Emerson and Henry David Thoreau, *Nature* and *Walking* (Boston: Beacon, 1994), 53.

AUTUMN

1. Thoreau, *Excursions,* 141.

Chapter 11: Trimming Trees

1. Thoreau, *Walden,* 79.

Chapter 12: Constructing Truth

1. Thoreau, *Walden,* 44.
2. Ibid., 41.

Chapter 13: Falling Apart

1. Quoted by Richardson, *Henry Thoreau,* 114 (see chap. 4, n. 5).

Chapter 14: Coyotes at the Mall

1. Thoreau, *Walden,* 218.
2. Quoted by Richardson, *Henry Thoreau,* 389.
3. See Stanley D. Gehrt, "Urban Coyote Ecology and Management: The Cook County, Illinois, Coyote Project," Ohio State University Extension, bulletin 929 (2006), http://urbancoyoteresearch.com/UrbanCoyoteManagement PDF.pdf.
4. Between 1973 and 1993, the annual Christmas count of the Canada goose in Chicago increased from 300 to 9,000, and the species was estimated to be increasing by 10–15 percent per year.
5. And, in doing so, they have also changed the behavior of geese. Researchers have found that adult geese that recognize the coyotes as lethal tend to stop fighting back against other animals they once overpowered. See the work of Ohio State University professor Stanley D. Gehrt, including the publication cited in note 3, above.

Chapter 15: The Art of Dying

1. Henry David Thoreau, *The Selected Works of Thoreau* (Boston: Houghton Mifflin, 1975), 793.

Chapter 16: Cougars in the Corn

1. Thoreau, *I to Myself,* 112.
2. See John G. Neihardt, *Black Elk Speaks: Being the Life Story of a Holy Man of the Oglala Sioux* (Lincoln: University of Nebraska Press, 2004).

WINTER

1. Thoreau, *Journal,* 687.

Chapter 17: A Familiar Darkness

1. Thoreau, *Walden,* 325.
2. Thoreau, *Journal,* 689.
3. Ibid., 690.
4. Ibid., 321.
5. Thoreau, *I to Myself,* 302.
6. The last line of Emerson's essay "Self-Reliance" echoes in Thoreau's life:

"Nothing can bring you peace but yourself. Nothing can bring you peace but the triumph of principles."

7. Jay C. Fournier et al., "Antidepressant Drug Effects and Depression Severity: A Patient-Level Meta-analysis," *Journal of the American Medical Association* 303, no. 1 (2010): 47–53.

8. This is, of course, partly due to scientific advances and redefinition of the "disorder," but the point is the same: people, in spite of increasing incomes, are more depressed and less "happy." See Richard Layard, *Happiness: Lessons from a New Science* (New York: Penguin, 2006), 36.

9. Thoreau, *Walden,* 30.

10. Joe Dominguez and Vicki Robin, *Your Money or Your Life: Transforming Your Relationship with Money and Achieving Financial Independence* (New York: Penguin, 1993).

11. Thoreau, *Walden,* 108.

Chapter 18: Traveling at Night

1. Thoreau, *I to Myself,* 122.

2. Thoreau, *Walden,* 95.

3. Ibid., 2.

4. Nicaragua is the second-poorest country in the western hemisphere after Haiti. Witness for Peace is a cross-cultural social-justice organization based in Washington, DC, with staff in Nicaragua, Colombia, and Mexico. In 1989, I was coleader of a WFP delegation to Guatemala.

5. Excerpted from Tom Montgomery Fate, *Anecdotes and Analysis from Nicaragua: Rice and Beans and Hope* (New York: Circus, 1988), 4–6.

6. Paul Theroux, *The Happy Isles of Oceania: Paddling the Pacific* (Putnam: New York, 1992), 18.

7. Thoreau, *I to Myself,* 73.

Chapter 19: Slow Pilgrim

1. Thoreau, *Excursions,* 107.

2. While seemingly authentic, this is an invented (false) etymology some historians think first circulated in Europe in the seventeenth century. The origins are uncertain.

3. Ibid., 105–6.

4. Or perhaps *I'm* trying to make a point. Note that this passage was written on April 1, April Fools' Day. Thus, *Homo sapiens* is *not* actually included in the *Audubon Field Guide.* The entry is invented, a farce. The brief definition is summarized from *Wikipedia.*

Credits

Thanks to the following publications, where these chapters (or excerpts) first appeared:

The *Chicago Tribune:* "A Familiar Darkness," "Fathers Watching Sons," and "Coyotes at the Mall."

Fourth Genre: Explorations in Nonfiction: "In Plain Sight," reprinted in *The Fourth Genre: Contemporary Writers of/on Creative Nonfiction,* 5th edition.

The *Iowa Review:* "Saunter."

Notre Dame Magazine: "Lake Glass" and "Fathers Watching Sons."

Orion: "The Art of Dying" and "Coyotes at the Mall."

Riverteeth: A Journal of Nonfiction Narrative: "A Box of Wind."

And thanks to the editors from these publications: David Hamilton, Marcia Lythcott, Joe Mackall, Colin McMahon, Jennifer Sahn, Michael Steinberg, and Kerry Temple.

Excerpts from "Picking Blackberries," "The Gay Cardinal," "Cabin Fever," "In the Time of the Cicada," "In Plain Sight," "Lake Glass," and "A Box of Wind" aired as separate essays on Public Radio International's *Living on Earth* program. Thanks to editor Eileen Bolinsky.

Excerpts from "The Art of Dying," "Deliberate Life," "Saunter," "Fathers Watching Sons," "A Box of Wind," and "Traveling at Night" aired as separate essays on Chicago Public Radio's *848* program. Thanks to editor Aurora Aguilar and producer Joe Deceault.